To Margaret
with love in
Glanfred Ch... ...nd
Mo ... ...t

D1321442

The Paschal Life

The Paschal Life

A series of daily meditations
from Easter to Pentecost
and also Trinity Sunday
and Corpus Christi

by

Marianne Dorman

The Pentland Press Limited
Edinburgh Cambridge Durham

© Marianne Dorman 1993
First published in 1993 by
The Pentland Press Ltd.
1 Hutton Close
South Church
Durham

ISBN 1 85821 016 X

Typeset by Print Origination (NW) Ltd., Liverpool
Printed and bound by Antony Rowe Ltd., Chippenham

To
The Glory of God
and
in thanksgiving
for the Glorified Life through Christ's
Living Spirit given to us in Baptism
and renewed daily in the Eucharist

I dedicate this book
to
Francis Martin and Basia
that, as they begin their married life,
the Living Christ will always abide
in their hearts

It is the Pasch; the Pasch of the Lord . . .
O You, who are truly all in all! . . .
The joy, the honour, the food and the delight of
every creature;
through You the shadows of death have fled away,
and life is given to all,
the gates of heaven are flung open.
God becomes man
and man is raised up to the likeness of God.

O divine Pasch! . . .
O Pasch, light of new splendour . . .
The lamps of our souls will no more burn out.
The flame of grace,
divine and spiritual,
burns in the body and soul,
nourished by the resurrection of Christ.

We beg You, O Christ, Lord God,
eternal king of the spiritual world,
stretch out Your protecting hands
over Your holy Church
and over Your holy people;
defend them, keep them, preserve them . . .

Raise up Your standard over us
and grant that we may sing with Moses
the song of victory,
for Yours is the glory and the power for all eternity! Amen.

A Paschal Hymn, based on
a tract on the *Pasch*
by Hippolytus, Bishop of Rome

Table of Contents

Foreword

Christians are essentially a "Resurrection People" and "Alleluia" is their song. Christians must not stop short at simply affirming the resurrection, on Easter Day. They need to celebrate the resurrection and incorporate it into their lifestyle.

The season of Easter, stretching from Easter Sunday through to Pentecost, is intended by the Church for such celebration. During the great Fifty Days we not only tell our story but we also celebrate its reality. The cry of the Church is one of praise and affirmation: "Christ is Risen! Alleluia! The Lord is Risen indeed! Alleluia!" We are a Red Sea people, who have been "through it", but already we are experiencing the end of the story here and now in the middle! It is sad that Christians in the West especially have concentrated upon the season of Lent to the exclusion or downgrading of the Paschal season. We need to tell our story again and again, in which actions speak louder than words and, enabled by the liturgy, to work out the implications of the overwhelming reality and historical fact of the Resurrection of Christ. All hope, enterprise and renewal spring from that fact which re-fashions the outlook and mind of the "Resurrection People".

Marianne Dorman has laid out a remarkably accessible programme of meditations and reflections which carry us through the great Fifty Days, leading to Pentecost and the fire of the Spirit to equip the Church for ministry and mission. With her detailed knowledge of the Fathers (especially the Eastern Fathers) she has peppered all her reflections with powerful imagery and memorable quotes. The book from start to finish both enlightens the mind and imagination, warms the heart and fires the will so that the lifestyle of Christian communities celebrating the resurrection eventually reflect that resurrection reality in day to day living.

Bishop Michael Marshall
13 September 1993

Preface

Christ is risen! Alleluia!
The Lord is risen indeed! Alleluia!

The great Fifty Days ring out with the glorious message of certain triumph over all earthly doom and despair because it has the message of life and vitality and the answer to all man's frustrations and fears. What more wonderful news could there be in all the world than that God the Son, born in very insignificant surroundings, and dying as a common criminal on a cross, is victor over all this world could do to Him, even death. By the Spirit the Father raised Christ from death, and thus the sting has been removed from the grave, and the risen Lord becomes 'a life-giving Spirit' (1 Cor. 15:45). The Resurrection rings out victory. As St. Paul reminds us, '*O Death, where is your sting?* The sting of death is sin, and sin gains its power from the law. But thanks be to God! He gives us victory through our Lord Jesus Christ.' (1 Cor. 15:55-7)

As St. Gregory Nazianzen, one of the great Cappadocian Fathers of the fourth century, exclaimed:

> Today is salvation come unto the world, to that which is visible, and to that which is invisible; Christ is risen from the dead, rise you with Him. Christ is returned again to Himself, return you. Christ is freed from the tomb, be you freed from the bond of sin. The gates of hell are opened, and death is destroyed, and the old Adam is put aside, and the New is fulfilled; if any man be in Christ he is a new creature; be you renewed.[1]

These glorious Fifty Days begin with the Easter Vigil Liturgy. On this great night we recall all the wonderful deeds God has done for His people in bringing them forth from darkness into His marvellous life. So the deacon chants:

> This is the night when the pillar of fire
> destroyed the darkness of sin!
> This is the night when Christians everywhere,
> washed clean of sin
> and freed from all defilement,
> are restored to grace and grow together in holiness.

The celebration of the Christian Pascha began very early amongst Christians, as early as the apostolic church. There is evidence of its liturgy in Paul's letter to the Ephesians:

> Awake, sleeper, rise from the dead,
> And Christ will shine on you.   (Eph. 5:14)

The importance of this night in the early church is again illustrated in this hymn by Gregory Nazianzen:

> But, O Pascha, great and holy and purifier of the world,
> for I shall speak to You as to a living person.
> O Word of God and Light and Life and Wisdom and
> Might,
> for I rejoice in all Your names.
> O Offspring and Expression and Signet of the Great
> Mind;
> O Word conceived and Man contemplated, Who bearest
> all things,
> binding them by the Word of Your power;
> receive this discourse, not now as first fruits,
> but perhaps as the completion of my offerings,
> a thanksgiving, and at the same time a supplication,
> that we may suffer no evil beyond those necessary
> and sacred cares in which our lives have passed,
> and stay the tyranny of the body over us.[2]

As mighty and wonderful as the Resurrection of Christ is, it is not complete nor effectual for us without the Ascension. The Jacobean prelate, Lancelot Andrewes, in his 1622 Easter Day sermon clearly demonstrates this:

The Resurrection itself is for an end, it is not the
end; it is but a state yet imperfect, but any entry to a
greater good which unless it leads us and brings us to,
'non habetur propositum', *it is short, short of that it
should be. . . . To rise is nothing but to ascend out of the
grave, . . . to rise as high as heaven, then we are truly
risen. . . . The Resurrection itself is no Gospel, not of
itself unless 'ascendo' follow it.*[3]

Christ had to return to His Father's home in order to fulfil His
promise to His apostles that He would always be with them. His
Ascension enabled the Holy Spirit to be poured out upon them and His
Church ever since. To realize the implication of all this we only have to
compare the lives of the apostles during the Resurrection days with
those after the Ascension. As we ponder on the events of that first
Pentecost morning we behold the power of the Spirit in transforming
and mending lives. Peter and the apostles simply cannot contain their
experiences of the Ascended Lord in their lives. Not only do they
desire to share this knowledge with others, but they ardently desire for
every man, woman and child to possess the Living Christ too. Peter
addresses the lame man at the Gate Beautiful with these words, 'I have
no silver or gold; but what I have I give you: in the name of Jesus Christ
of Nazareth, get up and walk.' (Acts 3:6)

The early Church manifested what it meant to live in the power of
the Risen and Glorified Lord. People repented and were baptized as
they responded to the preaching of the Gospel; they sold their goods
and lived communally; they prayed and celebrated the Eucharist daily;
they cared for one another through acts of charity. Their lives took on
that other dimension, that essential dimension of entering eternal life
now.

Wherever Christ is in this world, there are also found the gifts of the
Holy Spirit: humility, meekness, gentleness, long-suffering, patience,
temperance and above all love. It is only these attributes which bring
peace to a hostile world and heal the broken-hearted and the injured. It
is only through the power of the glorified Lord that each man, woman
and child can live without any fears whatsoever. Those who believe in
Christ are freed from any kind of yoke which strangles and finally kills.
Instead they savour that serenity and security of living within the

Kingdom of the Lord who reigns for ever and ever. Their lives do express that tremendous joy which rings out in the Easter Proclamation sung at the Easter Vigil Liturgy.

> Rejoice, heavenly powers! Sing, choir of angels!
> Exult, all creation around God's throne!
> Jesus Christ, our King, is risen!
> Sound the trumpet of salvation!
>
> Rejoice, O earth, in shining splendour,
> radiant in the brightness of your King!
> Christ has conquered! Glory fill you!
> Darkness vanishes for ever!
>
> Rejoice, O Mother Church! Exult in glory!
> The risen Saviour shines upon you!
> Let this place resound with joy,
> echoing the mighty song of all God's people!

It is important for us to realize that Pentecost is not a separate festival but the culminating celebration of these joyful Fifty Days during which we have truly experienced the liveliness of our faith. Nevertheless, Pentecost does have its own distinctive message with that new surging of energy, making hearts afresh and fearless. Just as the Christian *Pascha* is born out of the Jewish one, so the Christian Pentecost is rooted in the Jewish Feast of Weeks, held fifty days after the Passover when the first fruits of the harvest were offered to the Lord. St. Paul speaks of Christ being 'the first fruit'. Our Lord is not only the 'first fruit' for 'all who have fallen asleep' (1 Cor. 15:20) but the 'first fruit' of this new life begun with Calvary's victory. The more we ponder on Easter and Pentecost, the more we shall realize how intertwined these two celebrations are–Christ and the Holy Spirit with the Father are all united. This indeed unfolds as we read the set lessons for this time. It is no accident that we read side by side St. John's Gospel, with all its beauty and mystical appeal, uncloaking the harmony and unity of the Three in One, and One in Three, with *The Acts of the Apostles*, in which the real life experience of the blessed Trinity in the apostles' preaching and ministry are vividly presented by Luke.

The unity of all these are celebrated at the end of the *Feast of Weeks* on Trinity Sunday when the creative, redemptive and sanctifying works of God are all praised and honoured. On this day we give thanks for all

God's goodness as so aptly summed up in one of the loveliest prayers in the Book of Common Prayer, the *General Thanksgiving*: 'We bless You for our creation, preservation and all the blessings of this life, but above all for Your inestimable love in the redemption of the world by our Lord Jesus Christ, for the means of grace, and for the hope of glory.'

Often the Trinity is seen as being too complex for our understanding. How can God be one in three and three in one? Perhaps at no other time of the Christian year is it easier to see how the Three persons are One, and One in Three. As St. Irenaeus explained,

> 'the Lord redeems us . . . and pours out the Spirit of the Father to unite God and man. . . . The Word of The Father and the Spirit of God, united with the material substance of Adam, God's primal handiwork, had made man living and perfect, receptive of the Father.'[4]

The overwhelming joy of the great Fifty Days is that the Father, Christ and the Holy Spirit are always active. The Church is the Living Christ. Corpus Christi celebrated on the Thursday after Trinity Sunday honours that Living Christ and assures us that Christ and the Spirit are always present within the Church. After the gifts of bread and wine are placed on the altar, through the operation of the Holy Spirit (the epiclesis) they become the Body and Blood of the crucified and risen Lord.

The institution of the Eucharist has this special place of honour and celebration on Corpus Christi, even though we know it was instituted by Our Lord on Maundy Thursday. The reason for this is that the Passion of Our Lord, with its fast-moving events on Maundy Thursday through to Good Friday, in a sense dwarfs the institution of the Eucharist. Thus on this day we can truly express our thanks for the Bread of Life and the Cup of Salvation as we reverence our dear Lord in His most holy and wonderful Sacrament. On this day all over the world, processions are held to proclaim and praise Jesus as Lord in His Sacrament:

> Blessed and praised be Jesus Christ
> In the most holy Sacrament
> Hosanna, hosanna, hosanna in the highest!

Just as this series of meditations began with life, that new and risen life in Christ which transforms everything, so it ends with the gift of

Life, Christ's Body and Blood given to us day by day. Christ told us He is the 'Bread of heaven' and the 'Bread of Life', and as such He is our daily food for our pilgrimage towards heaven where I shall 'never, never part from You'.

This book follows on from my other meditative books, *The Coming of Christ* and *Living Lent*. My aim has been to enable the men and women of the pew to enter more fully into a more enriching and exciting experience of the meaning of the Risen and Glorified Lord in their lives. We are created to love God, now and for ever. That is our main vocation in life. However, we can only love God if we first respond to His love, and allow His love to fill our whole being. The Risen and Glorified Lord through the Spirit transforms everything and every person. In renewing and restoring us He makes us the people we were created to be, that is, to respond to the blessings we receive daily in the ongoing life of God's creation. Our lives overbrim with God's goodness, and we know we are surrounded at all times by the joys and wonders of the universe. The Risen and Ascended Christ is indeed Lord of the Cosmos!

The daily meditations are based on the readings for the daily Mass from Easter Day to Corpus Christi. The Sunday readings, except for the Third Sunday of Easter, are from Cycle A. All quotations from Scripture are taken from the Revised Standard Version of the Bible, and all quotations, except some poetry, are in modern English.

Oxford
St. John the Baptist 1993

---

[1] St. Gregory Nazianzen, *The Homilies of St. Gregory of Nazianzen* (Fathers of The Christian Church, Oxford, 1894), Vol. 7, pp.422-3.

[2] Ibid., pp.433-4.

[3] L. Andrewes, *The Works of Lancelot Andrewes*, eds. J. Bliss & J.P. Wilson, 11 vols. (The Library of Anglo-Catholic Theology, Oxford, 1841-1854), Vol. 3, p.46.

[4] H. Bettensen, *The Early Christian Fathers* (Oxford, 1990), p.88. Henceforth referred to as *Early Fathers*.

Acknowledgements

To the Australian National Botanic Gardens in Canberra for kind permission to use the transparency of *Eucalyptus concinna* for the cover.

To Harper Collins Publishers for permission to quote from *Hope and Suffering* by D. Tutu and *The Truce of God* by R. Williams.

To Longman Group U.K. for permission to quote from *The Works of The Fathers*, vols 1 and 6.

To Oxford University Press for permission to quote from *The Early Christian Fathers*, edited by H. Bettensen, 1990, and *The Later Christian Fathers*, edited by H. Bettensen, 1989.

To Paulist Press, New Jersey, U.S.A., for permission to quote from *Hildegard of Bingen*, edited by Mother Columba Hart and Jane Bishop, 1990.

To S.P.C.K. for permission to quote from *Praying with the Martyrs*, translation by D. Arnold, 1991; *Prayers for Peace*, edited by R. Runcie and B. Hume; *Holy Spirit*, Michael Ramsay; *Praying with The English Poets*, edited by R. Etchells; *The Power and Meaning of Love* by T. Merton.

To St. Paul's Publications for permission to quote from *To Him Be Praise*, edited by C. Berselli, and translated by Sister Mary of Jesus, O.D.C.

Easter Day

The Risen Lord

Then the disciple who had reached the tomb first also
went in, and he saw and believed; until then they had not
understood the scriptures, which showed that He must
rise from the dead.

St. John 20:8-9

Full readings: Acts 10:34, 37-43; Psalm 118; Colossians 3: 1-4; St. John
20: 1-9.

Today is the Queen of all festivals. Truly Easter is 'the Lord's
Passover, the Passover, and again I say the Passover to the honour of
the Trinity. This is to us, a Feast of feasts and a Solemnity of
solemnities, as far exalted above all others . . . as the Sun is above the
stars.'[5] So proclaimed Gregory Nazianzen, and no-one would disagree
with him. It is the most wonderful day of the year, there is not another
day like it, because this is the day when we are truly liberated from
everything negative: darkness, death, doubts, despairs, despondencies,
diseases, and all kinds of disharmonies. Our dear Lord and Saviour has
triumphed over all the worst that evil can do and manifest in this life. It
is victory over every conceivable corruptible aspect of life which now
enables us to aspire to all that is good, just and pure in this life. 'It is a
day the fullest of all good tidings, – as the seal and assurance of all the
good news we heard before it.'[6] This exuberance of Easter is captured
in the octet of this sonnet by Edmund Spenser.

Most glorious Lord of life, that on this day,
 didst make thy triumph over death and sin;
 and having harrowed hell didst bring away
 captivity thence captive, us to win:

1

This joyous day, dear Lord, with joy begin,
and grant that we for whom Thou diddest die
being with Thy dear blood clean washed from sin,
may live forever in felicity.[7]

It is a day when all fears, doubts and perplexities are driven from us.
As Mark Frank exclaims, 'This is a day when perplexities cannot stay,
fears cannot tarry with us, our heads cannot long hang down; the news
of it is so full of gladness, of comfort and joy.'[8]

It is a day indeed overbrimmed with joy. On what other day do we
feel so much joy? I am sure there is not another. On this day we explode with our happiness and gladness as we know that this earthly life,
although but transitory, is now full of hope and wonderful anticipation.
The eternal, which is already implanted in us, will no longer have to do
battle within us as we wrestle with all those worldly things which are
not part of God's kingdom. We know if we persevere in the power of
the Risen Christ in trying to overcome hatred with love, injustice with
kindness, deceit with honesty, cruelty with tenderness, and bitterness
with compassion, we shall enjoy for all eternity the wonders, joy and
bliss of being with our Glorified Lord. Today we are assured we too can
triumph over death and darkness through our crucified and now risen
Saviour. We are truly blessed!

For me, one of the most moving lines of scriptures is when the angel who is guarding the empty tomb announces to the women who have
come to anoint Christ's body with costly ointments and spices, 'He is
not here, for He is risen.' Transfiguration–everything has been made
anew. The old order has been replaced by the new. The old Adam in us
is supplanted by the new! In this newness is hope, happiness and holiness. The Resurrection has made all of life glorious and wonderful. All
is fresh; all is new; but all is eternal. 'I have come that you may have
life, and may it have abundantly,' rings out with every chime of every
bell we hear on Easter Day. Will we ever hear of a more comforting
message? Will we ever hear of a more dynamic message? No; after all,
'To whom should we go, You have the words of everlasting life.'

Easter assures us of eternal life; that eternal life begins when we are
baptized. Please never think of it as something which belongs to the
future. It is now with us. If we do not experience it along our earthly
pilgrimage, then we surely are not going to taste it later on. The
kingdom of God is within us, don't forget. The risen Lord lives within

us now, and draws us to Him closer and closer as we allow His Risen life to increase in us. Christ has risen! The Lord is risen indeed!

Easter further assures us that we shall henceforth live in the light because He Who is the Light of the world has eradicated all darkness. What wonderful gifts and blessings, which come from the Light of Christ, are manifested in this ancient hymn associated with Hilary of Poitiers.

> O resplendent giver of light,
> like lightning at Your command
> the time of darkness is past
> and daylight, regiven, spreads abroad.
>
> You are the true giver of light to the world,
> not as the tiny star,
> which, harbinger of the sun's rising,
> burns only with a feeble flame;
>
> but brighter than the fullest sun,
> all light and day,
> You light up the deepest sentiments
> of our hearts.
>
> Assist us, O Creator of the world,
> mirror of the light of the Father,
> for our flesh
> is fearful of losing Your grace.
>
> May chastity of mind
> overcome the shameful passions of the flesh,
> may the spirit preserve in holiness
> the temple of a body that is chastened.
> This is the hope of the soul in prayer,
> these the vows which we offer:
> that the light of the morning
> may persist even during the night.[9]

Today is the most wonderful day of the year. Thank you, dear Lord, for freeing me from all kinds of tyrannies through Your Resurrection.

May I continually praise You for the gift of eternal life and all the blessings which flow from Your triumph over death, disease and all kinds of disorders. Alleluia! Alleluia! The Lord is Risen. Christ is risen indeed and has triumphed over all the worst deeds that evil can do. Thanks be to God. Amen.

[5] St. Gregory Nazianzen, op. cit., p.423.

[6] M. Frank, *Sermons*, 2 vols. (Library of Anglo-Catholic Theology, Oxford, 1859), Vol. 2, p.84.

[7] E. Spenser, *Poetical Works* (Oxford, 1912), p.573.

[8] Frank, op. cit., p.84.

[9] C. Berselli, Ed., *To Him Be Praise*, trans. Sr. Mary of O.D.C. (Slough, 1982), pp.72-3.

Easter Monday

Boldness

Now Jesus has been raised by God, and of this we are all
witnesses.
Exalted at God's right hand He received from the Father
the promised Holy Spirit, and all that you now see and
hear flows from Him.

Acts 2:32-3

Full readings: Acts 2:14, 22-23; Psalm 16:1-2, 5, 7-11; St. Matthew
28:8-15.

Today's readings show the implication of the Risen Lord and His
Spirit within the lives of Christ's disciples. Their lives were suddenly
made glorious and enriching. Peter, who had sheepishly followed Jesus
after His arrest to Gabbatha and then, worse still, had denied ever
knowing Him, and as we saw yesterday peered into the empty tomb
without realizing the significance of this, is now filled with boldness,
such boldness that all intimidations, doubts and fear have vanquished.
He wants all those present on that first Pentecost morning to possess
what he and the other disciples have, this enriching and vivacious life in
Christ. Such they can have if they will believe that Jesus is alive as the
Risen Lord, and gives His potent life to all who repent and believe.

In that most powerful sermon at Pentecost Peter instructs his auditors
that, even if they had not seen Jesus during His earthly ministry, they
surely knew what had happened to Jesus in Jerusalem just prior to the
Passover when he had been condemned as a criminal to death by
crucifixion. It is this same Jesus who died at Golgotha, and who has
triumphed over the grave and all that evil could do, who is now risen
and glorified. In this glorified life, He fills His people with His power

and presence. However, Peter's bold proclamation met with much cynicism as many of his listeners felt that such an outrageous claim could only be made by someone who was drunk, even though it was very early in the morning.

Yet at the same time we know there were also many who were touched by the Spirit and received Peter's message wholeheartedly, and as a result repented of their sins and were baptized. They rose from the water of Baptism assured of the new life in the Risen Lord. In this new life, they formed the nucleus of the early church in Jerusalem, meeting constantly in prayer, Eucharist and teaching with the disciples. It was this remarkable boldness and fearlessness of Peter, Stephen, Phillip and other disciples which enabled the good news of Jesus to be sown in the hearts of many.

Are we bold about witnessing for Christ? If we are not, perhaps we have not allowed ourselves to receive the Risen Lord, let alone the Spirit which He sends as the culmination of the Resurrection. The stone was rolled away from the tomb in the Easter garden as a symbol that Jesus was no longer there, as He had risen. That stone in a sense represents the door to our hearts. Open the door and you will find the Risen Lord waiting to enter. Once we allow Him to come in, all kinds of wonderful things happen, one of which is being bold in Christ's name. The presence of the Holy Spirit does make us new people! He does direct our actions! He does speak through us! Like Peter we are no longer afraid to be true to Him and His teaching; we are no longer worrying about what others think of us. Our Lord had to despise the shame of the Cross in order to triumph over all that is sham in this world for us, for our eternal existence. St. Paul is also an inspiring example of being bold for Christ. Many times in his letters he spoke of being bold for Christ's sake, and, as he does in his second letter to the Corinthians, related the sufferings he gladly endured for such boldness (2 Cor. 11:21 ff.). Easter teaches us to be bold and brave, and the Spirit of the Risen Lord enables us to be so. Let us be Easter people.

Just as Peter boldly proclaimed the gospel news on Pentecost morning, let me also live boldly for You. O God, fill me with the power of the Risen Lord to quench all fears and faint-heartedness. Alleluia! Alleluia! The Lord is Risen. Amen.

Easter Tuesday

Noli Me tangere–Mary Magdalen

Jesus said, 'Mary!' . . .
'Do not cling to me,' said Jesus, 'for I have not yet
ascended to the Father. But go to my brothers, and tell
them that I am ascending to My Father and your Father,
to My God and Your God.'

St. John 20: 16-17

Full readings: Acts 2:36-41; Psalm 33:4-5, 18-20, 22; St. John 20:11-18.

Perhaps at first glance the first command to Mary Magdalen by the
Risen Lord may seem a little harsh. Harsh because Mary loved her
Lord very dearly, and was obviously quite distressed that she could not
find His body in the tomb on Easter morning for anointing with fresh
herbs and spices. However, when seen in the light of the second
command we are able to see the first in its right perspective. The second
command is the crucial one because it is outreaching and challenging; it
is for a far wider audience than just for one person. Mary was
commanded to tell the Gospel news that Jesus is alive to others; it was
not news simply for herself. Christ died on the Cross for every human
being. Therefore right at the outset it was not sufficient for Mary alone
to keep this wonderful news of the Risen Lord to herself. She was
privileged to be the first evangelist to relate the greatest event for
mankind, *Christ is risen!* This she shares with others immediately. The
disciples must know how important is the significance of the Lord rising
from death. What Jesus is challenging Mary with, and indeed us, is that
we cannot experience the Risen Lord in isolation; we must share it with
others as it belongs to all. Therefore, as Christians, we can only be truly
Christian if we share the Risen Lord with others. That of course means
not only sharing the knowledge that Christ is Risen, but the gifts we

receive as a result of all God's goodness and love to us. It's being a living cell in God's world. The gifts of Christ are boundless, unless we try to strangle them.

It should not be too difficult therefore to comprehend that what Our Lord expected of Mary Magdalen is what He also expects of us in proclaiming and living the Christian life. Really, there is no such thing as a Christian life unless we are prepared to share our experiences of being with Christ with others. Our message that the Lord is Risen and Ascended is given every time when we minister unto His people in this world by giving of ourselves when it hurts and bites into our cosy existence, when we absorb all the hurts and disappointments from others, and when we make decisions for Him and not for ourselves. Our Lord rightly says to us, '*Noli Me tangere*', until we have done the Lord's work.

How lavish we should be in our giving is also learnt from Mary of Magdala from whom Our Lord had cast out seven devils (Lk. 8:2). In being forgiven much, she loved much, and so one of the most tender, generous and selfless acts given to Jesus is when she washed and anointed His weary feet. Lancelot Andrewes catches the essence of this loving act in these words:

> And seeking by all means to express her *multam dilectionem propter multam remissionem... nothing she had was too dear. And having a precious ointment of nardus, the chief of all ointments, ... and in it too not of the leaf, but of the very choice part thereof, of the spike of the flower, ... that she did bestow. And that frankly, for she did not drop but pour; not a dram or two, but a whole pound; not reserving any, but breaking box and all; and that not now alone, but three several times, one after another.*[10]

Mary is not only our example in what giving is all about as a Christian, but in service too. No doubt she followed Him to Calvary and stood near the Cross on Good Friday, weeping bitterly at the sight of her Master being brought to such degradation. Yet it is in her early coming and seeking out Our Lord on Easter Day that she challenges us once again with our so often lethargic attitude towards seeking Christ, and of living each moment of each day with Him. Thus if we take

Mary's example seriously we are forced to ask ourselves, do we seek God at the beginning of each day? Do we get up early enough to spend time with Him before we have to tend to the daily routine? How often do I go out of my way to seek Him in others? It behoves us to recall that Mary set out very early in the morning to seek her Lord.

The challenge of the Resurrection is further presented to us in today's lesson. As we noted yesterday, Peter boldly proclaimed the Risen Lord to a large gathering on that first Pentecost morning. Yet it is not in his proclaiming of Christ's deeds which acutely draws our attention to his sermon but in his ardent desire that his listeners should possess what he and the other apostles have–that gift of potent life through the Spirit in Christ. In tomorrow's lesson we shall see in a more remarkable way how Peter and John shared their wonderful gift of Christ's love, and what can happen if we first believe that Christ is Risen. In His Resurrection He has blessed us with healing power to conquer all disease and disorder and division. If only we would believe this, as Mary of Magdala did, then the Spirit of this Risen Lord would abound in this world!

As You challenged Mary Magdalen with the meaning and implementation of the Resurrection, so challenge me, dear Risen Lord. Let me firmly believe that I must always share the knowledge of and the benefits from Your Resurrection with others. Let this Risen life glow from me. Christ is Risen! Alleluia! Amen.

[10] Andrewes, op. cit., Vol. 2, p.38.

Easter Wednesday

Emmaus

Then their eyes were opened, and they recognized Him; but He vanished from their sight. They said to one another. 'Were not our hearts on fire as He talked with us on the road and explained the scriptures to us?'

St. Luke 24:31-32

Full readings: Acts 3:1-10; Psalm 105:1-4, 6-9; St. Luke 24:13- 35.

I always feel that the *Emmaus* episode is like a self-confession because it is so much like an average situation all over the world. While Cleopas and his friend are travelling to Emmaus they are doing what we precisely so often do, chatting away about the latest happenings in the neighbourhood. Jesus joins them, and enquires what it is that is so engrossing them. So, sadly, they inform Him of the horrible death of the One they had believed in as their Saviour. There was no bitterness or back-biting about their reply, but as they were so filled with their own feelings of grief, they could not recognize who had joined them, and hear what He was really saying.

How often are we guilty of this same situation? We are so caught up with our own little world and friends and often with the trivia of life that we are oblivious of others, let alone any plight they may be in. We don't really see people; we don't really listen; we don't really care!

This journey to Emmaus can also be seen as a picture of the parish church. We can be so caught up with going to church, attending the Parish Council, organizing the parish fête, leading a discussion group that we ignore completely in whose name we are doing these activities. We can be so busy being busy that we never have time to ask ourselves why are we doing this? The Emmaus episode of Easter challenges us to ask whether we see and recognize the Risen Lord in all our undertakings. The good news from the day's walk for these two disciples was that eventually the Stranger did awaken them from themselves, but only after Jesus deliberately chose to act in a way that it made it almost impossible to remain uninvolved. As they sat to share a meal at the end of the day, the disciples were challenged by Jesus as He blessed, broke and offered the bread. Now they see this Stranger for who He is; now, after being with Him, they recognize Him as their Lord; now they begin to ponder on the conversation they had with Him along the road to Emmaus. What the Stranger had been telling them was so true; Jesus had indeed fulfilled the Scriptures. Encountering the Risen Christ changes their attitude immediately. No longer do they feel sorry for themselves, but are filled with a burning desire to hurry back to their friends and proclaim this most glorious news, that Christ is indeed alive. Their encounter with Christ makes them abandon their preoccupation with self and to think of others. They do not return the same people!

In a sense, to grow in the Christian life, we all have to walk our road to Emmaus. However we walk it, we all have to encounter the Risen Lord at the end of it. But will we recognize Him at the end? Even when He gives a great sign? Will our hearts burn zealously for Him when we do recognize Him? Will we hasten back to our abode and proclaim Him in our changed style of living? A true Emmaus encounter becomes a watershed in our Christian lives. We can only go forward, living in His presence and through His life-giving spirit.

Another important lesson from today's Gospel reading is that, when the three had reached Emmaus, Jesus intimated that He would travel further. Travelling with Jesus always involves going further. Living the Christian life demands that we always go further than our non-Christian friends would sometimes go, in every situation and encounter. Love goes the extra mile all the time; Love turns the other cheek all the time; Love gives until it costs something all the time; Love never holds back; Love never keeps part for oneself. Do walk your Emmaus road this Easter, and recognize Your Risen Lord along it!

As I walk my road to Emmaus this Eastertide, help me not to ignore You in those I meet along the way. Let me never be so preoccupied that I am always blinkered. Let me be challenged by my encounter with You, so that I do not return as the same person. Amen.

Easter Thursday

Fulfilling the Law and Prophets

'So you see,' [Jesus] said, 'that scripture foretells the sufferings of the Messiah and His rising from the dead on the
third day.'

St. Luke 24:46

Full readings: Acts 3:11-26; Psalm 8:2, 5-9; St. Luke 24:35-48.

Before that first Easter Day came to an end, the Risen Lord
appeared before many of the disciples who were still obviously quite
perplexed about all the strange things which had happened that day.
The Gospel for today begins with Cleopas and his friend telling the
assembled and frightened disciples what had happened on their journey
to Emmaus. While they are talking about their encounter with the
Risen Lord He stood before them. At first they were aghast. What kind
of apparition was this which had come to torment their already
distressed spirits? Unlike His direct command to Mary Magdalen,
Christ has to reassure the huddled disciples that He is alive before He
can give them any command. Thus He demands that they reach out and
touch Him, and feel His wounded and torn hands and feet. They must
be certain that the Christ who died upon the Cross is ALIVE, and that
He has conquered the worst that this world can do!

Contrary to His attitude towards Mary as He challenges her with
taking the Good News to others, Our Lord here knows that the
disciples cannot deliver such News until their faith has been restored in
Him. Therefore He follows His old pattern of patiently teaching them.
Didn't they realize that what had transpired these last three days had all
been foretold in the Law and the Prophets? If only they had believed
the Scriptures! If only they had believed His teaching to them! He had

forewarned them: 'Destroy this temple,...and in three days I shall raise it up again!' (Jn. 2:19). Oh, how slow of heart they were, just as we are so often!

That their faith in Him as the fulfiller of the Law and Prophets is restored is evident in the lessons for this week. Peter, as we have seen, boldly proclaims Jesus as fulfilling the Scriptures as the promised Messiah who would redeem His people. Just as the Risen Lord on that first Easter Day instigates faith in the disciples, so do they likewise in others after Our Lord's ascension and His sending His Spirit. We see this in the lame man by the temple gate who is given the gift of faith after his healing by Peter and John.

Our Lord appearing in His Risen body to the disciples also signifies that nothing can be the same again. The Old Covenant is superseded by the New; the Jewish Laws are enriched by the command to love; and Sunday replaces the old Sabbath as the main day of worship and recreation; indeed every Sunday is a mini-Easter. The lives of the disciples are no longer the same; they are changed men through the Spirit sent to them by the Risen Christ. No longer are they timid, but bold; no longer fearful, but confident; no longer depressed, but vivacious.

Once the living and Risen Christ has touched our lives, nothing is the same again either. If our lives do not change dramatically, then it is a fair sign that the Risen Lord has not been able to penetrate through all our layers of selfishness and self-conceit and arrogance. We are still at the level of our idea of being a Christian. Cardinal Newman once said, 'To live is to change.' How true, because if we are not changing, if our lives are in a comfortable rut, what is actually happening is that we are slowly dying. One morning we shall awake and discover that we are dead! Only the Risen Lord can deliver us from this dying. By allowing the Spirit to enter and possess our lives, we are awakened, we are alert; we are attentive. We are alive in Christ, and in that aliveness our lives are constantly changing. When we endeavour to do the Lord's work, it is exciting too, because we don't know what we shall be doing this time next week as we surrender ourselves to the direction of the Holy Spirit.

I know there are many who panic very easily if they do not have a set schedule. Such people want to feel in command of every situation; they have not learnt that whoever will find his life must lose it. However, for those of us who allow Christ to be the Commander, our not knowing the future is not distressful at all; a Christian soon learns there is no such thing as a neat plan of life, and if a plan is made, how often is it torn up in shreds! If you are still a person who has not learnt to let go, and who finds the idea of not being able to organize the future frustrating and distressful, my advice simply is, do not cling, but live out the message of the Gospel. Do what Christ told Mary Magdalen on that first Easter Day. The Resurrection message is all about change, challenge and courage. As I write this I am reminded of the prayer we took as our College motto:

> Give me serenity to accept what cannot be changed,
> Courage to change what should be changed,
> And the wisdom to know the one from the other.

Just as the Risen Lord appeared before His disciples on Easter Day to assure them of His promises, may we too at this Eastertide be assured that His promise of always being with us is the only security we need as we live out the challenge the empty tomb gives us.

Implant that living Spirit, O Risen Christ, within me, so that I may confidently live out each day what You desire, and go wherever You lead. May I believe that to live fully is to be constantly changing and being challenged. Amen.

Easter Friday

The Cornerstone

They brought the apostles before the court and began to interrogate them. 'By what power', they asked, 'or by what name have such men as you done this?' . . .
'This is our answer to all of you and all people of Israel: it was by the name of Jesus Christ of Nazareth. . . . This Jesus is the stone, rejected by you the builders, which has become the cornerstone. There is no salvation through anyone else.'

Acts 4:7, 10-12

Full readings: Acts 4:1-12; Psalm 118:1-2, 4, 22-27; St. John 21:1-14.

We all probably realize that the *cornerstone* is the indispensable part of any building. Without it a building would collapse or at least be shaky, as it forms the spot where two sides join together. Our Lord Jesus Christ, as Peter informs the Jewish authorities in today's lesson, is THE cornerstone. However, they dismissed Jesus as the stone, when they rejected His teaching, and worse still when they crucified Him. 'Before they had cast Him aside, this poor Stone, they hacked and hewed it and mangled it piteously.'[11] If only they had believed that this stone would form the cornerstone! Yet their refusal had already been foretold in today's psalm. 'The stone which the builders rejected has become the main cornerstone.' (Ps. 118:22)

Peter in proclaiming Christ as the cornerstone was stating that through His Resurrection He is the foundation for every building, that is, for every soul in this world. 'Had He not risen we had had no ground to build upon; . . . neither place for faith, nor ground for hope, nor room for preaching; . . . all come to nothing.'[12] Thus it is His Spirit after His

15

Resurrection which pours life into every being, just as they had witnessed in the healing of the crippled man. Without the solidity of the chief Stone, our lives become like the builder who built his house on sand.

This means basically that we live very superficially and shallowly, and often very introspectively. We mostly lack that vision to reach out, to accept challenges and embrace life. It also means we have nothing for support when we face the tribulations and trials of this life. We are indeed anchorless.

Our Lord, in being the Cornerstone, also signifies He is the meeting place, the place of union for all and everything. Just as God and Man meet in Jesus Christ, so do Jew and Gentile, male and female, black and white, free and bound, poor and rich, teacher and pupil, employer and employee, and priest and people. Today's readings, emphasizing Christ as the Cornerstone, should make us aware of our one brotherhood in Christ where all are equal. There should never be any feeling of inferiority or superiority amongst Christians. We are meant to share the gifts we have been given with each other. They are never to be squandered on ourselves, and never are we to think that what we do is better than the next person. It can only be better in the sense that we are doing it for God, in the belief it is part of God's will for us.

The Cornerstone should also make us re-examine our attitude towards the unity of Christ's body in this world, the Church. Is it something we fervently desire? Something for which we pray each day? Or do we have a cosmetic approach to it? That is, spasmodic prayers with members of another denomination. However, if we take Christ seriously, it should be something we yearn and pray for, and work towards.

There is also another very special way in which the Cornerstone is a meeting place: in the Passover of the Jewish church and the Eucharist of the Christian church. Andrewes in his 1611 Paschal sermon illustrates this point so well:

> One chief corner-point of His was, 'when He joined the Lamb of the Passover and the Bread of the Eucharist, ending the one and beginning the other, recapitulating both Lamb and Bread into Himself'; making that Sacrament,

by the very institution of it, to be as it were the very cornerstone of both the Testaments.[13]

It is indeed in this Eucharist that we make our corner with Him. Our Lord gives us His Life, and our spiritual Food each day as we kneel at the altar rail. Here we are reminded of St. John's words:

Whoever eats my flesh and drinks my blood dwells in me and I in Him. As the living Father sent me, and I live because of the Father, so whoever eats me will live because of me. (Jn. 6:56-7)

Let us at this Paschal time make sure that we join our lives with Christ's at the holy Eucharist, and so form the cornerstone for our lives and living.

Through Your Resurrection You are the foundation for our very existence. Let me not be like the builder who rejected the chief stone, but rather let me be so joined to You that I form a secure corner. Amen.

---

[11] Andrewes, op. cit., Vol. 2, p.277.
[12] Frank, op. cit., Vol. 2, p.121.
[13] Andrewes, op.cit., Vol. 2, p.288.

Easter Saturday

Transformation

'What are we to do with these men?' they said. 'It is common knowledge in Jerusalem that a notable miracle has come about through them; and we cannot deny it.'

Acts 4:16

Full readings: Acts 4:13-21; Psalm 118:1, 14-21; St. Mark 16:9-15.

A few days ago we considered the boldness of Peter on that first Pentecost morning. That boldness was a result of his life being transformed. Easter, together with Pentecost, means that.

If we have kept Lent aright, we have endeavoured to strip ourselves of all pretensions; we have examined our lives and acknowledged our sins and what sin does to our very existence. In a sense we have become naked, and stand like a tree in winter, unclothed. Just as the bare limbs stretch upwards, waiting most patiently to be clad once again and to glory in the renewal of life, so we too await Easter morn to be clothed in white and receive the pulsating life of Christ.

With the life of the Risen Lord within us, we go out from our Easter Communion to live out the meaning of Easter in all our avenues of living. The Risen Lord assures us that even the humdrum existences of life take on new meaning. Nothing should be seen as a menial task; everything we do is of equal importance; and every aspect of life is meaningful and purposeful. All of life is transformed through the power of the Resurrection.

Just as our Lord told Mary Magdalen to go and tell the disciples that He had risen, so He addresses us in the same way. We proclaim His Resurrection every time we triumph over our pride, indifferences, slothfulness, greed and selfishness, our hanging on to the trivia of this world, our lack of concern for our neighbours, and our failures in standing up for justice and truth.

In today's lesson the Jewish authorities acknowledged this transformation in the lives of the followers of Jesus. They hardly could not recognize an obvious healing of this crippled man who had probably sat at the temple gate for years, but they were at their wits' end as to how to stop such miracles. If only they had realized men cannot stop the work of God; hinder perhaps, but never sever. This is precisely Peter's response to the authorities, as he immediately praised God for the transformations taking place in His name.

Easter reassures us we have been given the potential to be restored to our former glory before 'all was sin and shame'. Christ wants us to reach out and tap that potential; He did not die an agonizing death simply for us to say, 'thank you very much' and not do anything about it. He wants us to come, in the words of St. Paul, 'to mature manhood, measured by nothing less than the full stature of Christ' (Eph. 4:13). This is what our transformation means, to become a complete person, confident in Our Lord, and assured that His grace is always sufficient for us to transform our sinful nature and any situation. He had made all things new. Easter means 'a new order has begun' (2 Cor. 5:17). Let us show our heartfelt thanks to our Risen Saviour by discarding the old person and putting on the new. Let us wear our new white garment to glorify Christ and to manifest the power of the Resurrection in how we live each day. Our transformation should be similar to that of nature depicted by this medieval Welsh poet in *May and January*.

> And great, by Mary, will be
> That flawless month, May, 's coming,
> Intent, hot for his honour,
> On conquering each green glen.
> Close cover, cloak of highways,
> Clothes each place in its green web.
> When the war with frost is past,
> Meads flourish, thick-leaved mantles,
> Green will be, my credo chirps,
> May's paths, no longer April's,
> Then will come to the oak-tops
> The cheeping of baby birds,
> Cuckoos in every quarter,

And songsters, and long fine days,
And white mist, the wind dying,
Shielding the heart of the glen,
Then come bright skies, fine evenings,
Lovely trees, green gossamer,
And many birds in the woods,
And fresh leaves on the branches,
And thoughts of my gold Morfudd
And the three-score turns of love.[14]

We are called to be Easter people as Christ, through His death and Resurrection, has transformed us from our corruptible existence into an incorruptible one. We celebrate Easter with so much joy and festivity, not only in honour and thanksgiving for Our Lord's triumphant victory over sin, death and all evil, but for our freedom from bondage of these. In Christ we are now free people. No wonder we explode with our *Te Deum* during the great Fifty Days! Indeed the joy we feel is uncontainable—just as it was for Peter and the other disciples in today's lesson. In fact, the force of this explosive joy is in direct contrast to the almost melancholic version of the Resurrection attributed to St. Mark's as today's Gospel reading.

My Risen Saviour, You have freed me from slavery of sin and all evil. Give me Your grace to be that new person, and to come to the fullness of my potential. Thanks be to You for the victory You have gained over all darkness and death. Alleluia, alleluia. The Lord is Risen! Amen.

[14] J. P. Clancy, ed. *Medieval Welsh Lyrics* (London, 1965), p.86. Hereafter referred to as *Medieval Lyrics*.

The Second Sunday of Easter

Doubting Thomas

'Unless I see the marks of the nails on his hands, unless I put my finger into the place where the nails were, and my hand into His side, I will never believe it.'

St. John 20:25

Full readings: Acts 2:42-47; Psalm 118; 1 Peter 1:3-9; St. John 20:19-31.

How often are we a *doubting Thomas*? So often wanting a sign of God's presence, or some assurance that we are doing His will, or indeed that He even exists. We mistrust God because our prayers for a very ill friend have not been answered as we demanded, or we disown Him because an innocent child has been killed by a speeding motorist. Like Thomas, we have not understood His discourse on 'I am the true vine' and we 'are the branches', meaning that He abides in us and we in Him (Jn. 15:1 ff.). He has readily assured us that, if we live in Him and His word dwells within us, we may 'ask whatever [we] want, and [we] shall have it' (Jn. 15:70).

Oh, how little is our faith, no more than Thomas' when he demanded visible proof before he would believe that Christ was risen. We know from today's Gospel that Thomas was given his proof. Perhaps we may think Thomas lucky; Christ has never appeared before me, we murmur. Yet if we pause for a moment, and be not so hasty in our judgment, we might catch a glance of Him. He may be in the person for whom we prayed to be healed physically if we but look; He may be quite evident in the next person we encounter; and He may unveil something of Himself next time we give time to listen to Him.

Not many of us have encounters like St. Thomas or St. Paul, or even St. Francis of Assisi, with their Lord, but that does not say we do not have encounters with him. If we look back through our lives, we should be able to recall many, many encounters, some very little and some much bigger, that we have had with our Master. And if we but ponder long enough we shall see how they have been part of shaping our lives. Many of us have experienced situations where decisions have been taken out of our hands, or we have ended up doing something quite differently from what we had planned, and sometimes find we cannot explain why. Are not these encounters with God?

Furthermore, not many of us will be granted an apparition of Christ during our earthly pilgrimage, but haven't we been able to behold Him often through our spiritual senses? This is the point that Andrewes makes in his 1613 Nativity sermon when he asserts that Abraham in Mamre through faith beheld the Christ Child just as real as Simeon did in His arms.[15] In our times of quietness, stillness, and as we go about our everyday living, His presence can be very real; so much so, that we want to turn and touch Him.

Yet in this whole episode with Thomas, I don't really believe that the crucial point is in Thomas's disbelief or belief, but in what Our Lord says to Thomas. Firstly, He directs him to feel His wounds in order to believe in Him. What our Lord is telling Thomas here, and us too, is that we can never be His disciples without the Cross. Secondly, Jesus instructs Thomas in the essence of believing: 'Because you have seen me you have found faith. Happy are they who find faith without seeing me' (Jn. 20:29). Our Lord is also saying these words to us. Our very relationship with God is built on faith; and that is why we so often pray, 'increase my faith'. As our faith becomes more and more real and meaningful, so does God and our seeing and hearing of Him. I think all of us are familiar with the *Breastplate of St. Patrick*, but I would like us to reflect once again on it because it is the epitome of faith:

> Christ with me,
> Christ before me,
> Christ behind me,
> Christ in me;
> Christ under me,

Christ over me,
Christ to the right of me,
Christ to the left of me;
Christ in lying down;
Christ in sitting,
Christ in rising up;
Christ in the heart of everyone who thinks of me;
Christ in the mouth of everyone who speaks to me;
Christ in every eye who sees me;
Christ in every ear who hears me.

Pray that each day, or whenever we are sceptical, and I am sure it will restore our faith and our being able to see Christ in our lives, in others and in His world.

Of course, there is nothing wrong with having doubts, or even disbelieving at times as they can be times of growth. As we read the lives of many of the saints we know that they experienced doubts, mistrusts, and even loss of faith. Indeed there are some like St. John of the Cross who believed that the soul needed to experience these forms of darkness in order to purify the soul in its quest for union with God. So never panic when we do have moments of doubts, only panic if we do not see them as a means of strengthening our faith and our trust in the Risen Lord with His promise of fullness of life in the Spirit.

Let me stretch forth my hand in faith to You, dear Lord, knowing that at this Eastertide I shall be richly renewed by Your ever-abiding presence and life in the Paschal Supper. All praise and thanks be to You for all the benefits I have gained through Your death and Resurrection. Amen.

[15]Andrewes, op. cit., Vol. 1, pp.128-30.

Monday after the Second Sunday of Easter

Healing

'And now, O Lord, mark their threats, and enable those who serve You to speak Your word with all boldness. Stretch out Your hand to heal and cause signs and portents to be done through the name of Your holy Servant Jesus.'

Acts 4:29-30.

Full readings: Acts 4:23-31; Psalm 2:1-9; St. John 3:1- 8.

One of the very first signs of the Risen Lord being manifested in the Apostolic Church was in the healing ministry. No sooner had the apostles received the Spirit than its power was manifested in the healing of the crippled man outside the Temple gate, and the sick who were brought to them.

We know from Our Lord's own ministry that healing is at the very centre of it, both physically and spiritually. As it was in Christ's time, so it should be in ours. He came to give wholeness. The Church exists to continue His ministry and therefore healing must form a central part, otherwise it is not fulfilling Christ's command. This world is full of people crying out for healing: the brokenhearted, the downtrodden, the frightened, the rejected, and all enslaved by sin and guilt. They, and we, all need to know the power of Jesus in their and our lives. It is that power alone which heals and mends and makes anew.

Each Christian is called to a ministry of reconciliation; it is the one

ministry we all share in common; it is the Christian who must endeavour to reconcile and bring acceptance amongst those who are
divided for whatever reason. There is no room in the life of a Christian
for such attitudes as: *I really cannot get on with that person*, or *it's not
my responsibility to look after him or her.* Granted we may find some
people difficult or not sharing similar outlooks, but that has nothing to
do with getting on with another or shirking responsibility. In Christ,
through His death and Resurrection, we are all brothers and sisters.
Therefore, for example, if there are divisions within families and/or
parish communities we do something positive about them. In some
ways a Christian acts as a bridge by endeavouring through prayer and
loving listening and action to heal the faction. Often this is no easy task,
as many factions are caused by deep-seated fears, prejudices and
dislikes. Yet if we genuinely believe in the effectiveness of prayer and
that God desires so much that each person be freed of any kind of
slavery, then we shall persevere.

  Of course, much of the brokenness in this world is not on our
doorsteps. That does not say we cannot get involved. Included in our
daily petitions should be a fervent offering up to God of all the hatred,
bitterness, brutality, torture, unforgiveness and retaliation throughout
this broken world. Our Lord's body was broken on the Cross in order
to heal this broken world, and we must never forget that. That should
be our daily prayer. I am sure if more Christians genuinely prayed for
reconciliation amongst all peoples each day, then this would happen.
Recall what Peter said to the cripple, 'I have no silver or gold; but what
I have I give you: in the name of Jesus Christ of Nazareth, get up and
walk' (Acts 3:6).

  All of these kinds of brokenness stem from a sense of sin and guilt.
For healing to take place in any torn community or individual, there
must be penitence and contrition for sin and a confession of them. Only
then can the healing grace of God penetrate and make whole.

  Obviously Christians cannot be healing agents, if we ourselves are
not whole persons; and if we are still enslaved by forms of guilt, fears,
tremblings, uncertainties, hatred, revenge, anger and so on. This means
that to be open to the healing work of the Spirit we must constantly
examine our lives and repent of our sins and strive with God's grace to
overcome them once we have received forgiveness. This freeing gives
room for the Spirit, and the manifestations of it such as love, patience,
perseverance and hope which are so necessary in the ministry of

healing. So important is the forgiveness of sin in healing that one of Our Lord's first charges to the disciples on that first Easter was to give them authority in His name to forgive or retain sin. We have to learn to live positively.

Healing, as today's Gospel indicates, is part of the process of our rebirth in the life of the Spirit. This begins in the waters of Baptism. The affirming of our Baptismal vows a week ago at the Easter Vigil should still be fresh in our minds. Although the inclusion of Baptism as one of the essential parts of the Easter Vigil Liturgy does not today have the same impact as it did in the early church, when the catechumens underwent a long preparation during Lent, and on Easter Eve descended the waters of Baptism on one side and ascended on the other side, signifying a new beginning, nevertheless Baptism should still symbolize for us the putting on of Christ's robe and fighting against all the powers of darkness in this world and being blessed by His gifts. In Baptism we are healed as the cleansing water removes all stains of sin, and made whole persons. 'Risen with healing in His wings' is surely one of the great messages of Easter.

Dear Lord, You died on the Cross to heal all brokenness within Your world. Give me grace to be an instrument of Your healing so that Your work of reconciliation may continue through me. Let me always seek to mend rather than to tear, to forgive rather than to hold grudges, to evaluate rather than to judge, and above all give me a heart full of love. Amen.

Tuesday after the Second Sunday of Easter

Barnabas and Communism

Not one of them claimed any of his possessions as his
own; everything was held in common.... There was
never a needy person among them, because those who
had property... would sell it, bring the proceeds of the
sale,... to be distributed to any who were in need.

Acts 4:32, 34-35

Full readings: Acts 4:32-7; Psalm 92:1-2, 5; St. John 3:7-15.

Communism as a way of living in the Western world has always been
treated rather contemptuously, especially in the twentieth century,
because of its association with Marxism, and its obvious corruption and
cruelty as expressed under certain regimes. George Orwell certainly
exposed this in his satiric novel *Animal Farm*. The *iron curtain* across
Europe was certainly no myth!

Yet in reality communism lived out is the Christian gospel, because it
is a system by which all members of a community work for the common
good and benefit, and share whatever they have with their fellow members. It is this system which the early church practised, and so in today's
lesson we see how Barnabas and the early Christians sold their possessions so that all wealth could be shared amongst them all. Nothing was
held back because nothing was considered to be *mine*. Hence the early
church is 'united in heart and soul'; there is no division of any kind as
all are bonded in this one desire to bear 'witness to the Resurrection of
the Lord Jesus'.

How often today do we hear adults and children squabbling, or worse still fighting, because something or some person is regarded as *mine*. Possession, possessions and more possessions of these worldly goods are pursued with such greed and speed by so many. Yet what does it achieve? Happiness? No, because we are never satisfied with what we have; we want more and more of these worldly goods. Health? No guarantee, even of that, as wealth is not an insurance policy against sickness. Security? Even that is uncertain, as the present economic climate is a grim reminder. So what I believe is *mine* by right is not right after all.

What is right? The Gospel tells us today that we have to 'be born again' in the Spirit (Jn. 3:7-8). This means we become subjects of His kingdom, and we live according to the laws of Christ's kingdom. Within that kingdom there is no such thing as *mine*, but there is such a thing as *ours*. All that we have is a gift from God; we don't really possess anything. Newman expresses this rather wonderfully when he says our 'worldly lot and worldly goods are a sort of accident of... existence, and that [we] really have no property.'[16] All is for communal use. That is why we cannot be Christians in isolation; we belong to a community bonded in the death and Resurrection of Christ. Within that community we share, and gladly share, what we have of property, talent, wealth, time and energy with others. As we receive so much from others every day of our lives, we thank our God daily for meeting our needs. 'It is good to give thanks to the Lord, to sing [praises] to Your name, Most High' (Ps. 92:1). As we try to live in this communal way we realize too just how much we are dependent on others, and how much more our lives are enriched by them. Communal living makes us learn how to receive gladly as well as giving cheerfully.

Communism as expressed in countries dominated by Lenin and his successors failed eventually because it can only really work where all are in one accord and one mind under Christ. It is Christ who makes all things communal, not man. Thus one has to live in Christ and with Christ for communism to be effective. It is His living Spirit within which unites all in loving sharing and concern. When He is not present it does not work, as we discover when we continue to read on in Acts. Here in Chapter Five we see the results of the connivings of Ananias and Sapphira. If we follow the example of this husband and wife, we are no longer living within the kingdom of God, and we become victims of this world with all its ugly manifestations.

Thus, if we truly want to be Easter people, we must learn to be part of Christ's community, and live accordingly. You will discover riches and freedom you have never dreamed of because you are no longer enslaved by anything. Christ's death and Resurrection have really set you free. You are a free person in Christ, which means you can be the person God wants you to be.

You came to liberate us from all kinds of enslavements, dear Saviour, deliver me from any kind of possessiveness. As a member of Your community let me cheerfully share all the gifts You have given me. Help me to learn both to give and receive generously. Amen.

[16] J.H. Newman, *Parochial and Plain Sermons*, 8 vols. (London, 1868), Volume 4, p.326.

Wednesday after the Second Sunday of Easter

Freedom

During the night, an angel of the Lord opened the prison doors, led them out, and said, 'Go, stand in the temple and tell the people all about this new life.'

Acts 5:19-20

Full readings: Acts 5:17-26; Psalm 34:2-9; St. John 3:16-21.

The apostles had been arrested and imprisoned because of the impact of their preaching. All manifestations of healings and newness of life were being done in the name of Christ and the religious authorities had become alarmed and frightened. Their answer was to lock the apostles in gaol, hoping to put an end to it all, but the work of God cannot be put away as we do a new dress or suit for a special occasion. The authorities had also underestimated the unswerving trust the apostles had in their Lord. This trust enabled them to be free of all selfish desires and needs, with only a humble desire to do God's will. Thus they knew that God would not desert nor fail them, as His power within them was all too real.

When the angel led them outside the prison doors in the depth of night, it was as if the apostles expected it. This certainty was cemented when the angel instructed them to continue their preaching on 'this new life'. So where do we find them at dawn? In the temple! We have to look no further than the Gospel for today to know what they preached. God sent His Son into the world to give eternal life to those who believed in Him. As He is also the Truth, they who follow Him will know that 'God is in all they do.' And those like the religious leaders of Jerusalem will never know Truth as they prefer to live in their own darkness (Jn. 3:21).

I cannot stress too much how one of the important messages of Easter is freedom. We are free people. Will it never penetrate our thick skulls? Christ's Resurrection sets us free from everything which separates us from Him, and our complete absorption in Him. Oh, how so many of us are weighed down and enslaved to and by the values of this world. When shall we realize they are nothing in comparison with 'His service which is perfect freedom'?

Why do you think Christ died for us, and such an agonizing death into the bargain, if it were not to be free? He did not die for us to continue living in a slavish way unto sin and self but to be a living organism. He absorbed all sin as He died at Golgotha, and in His Resurrection released us from this old bondage. 'There is a new creation: the old order has gone; a new order has already begun.' (2 Cor. 5:17).

With this freedom we can begin to live with the same expectations as the apostles had. Once we realize it is only God who is our Master, and for Him we live, then we expect great things to happen in our Christian living. Just as the apostles were freed from imprisonment, so our chattels are severed. We discover riches and blessings that hitherto we never dreamed were possible. Allowing ourselves to be free in the Lord's service each day brings a new dimension to our everyday experiences. There is always something wonderful and enriching in each day. Of course, being free in the Lord does not mean we sit and wait for these wonderful experiences to happen; what it does mean is that, in being prepared to spend and be spent, we never end up losing; there is always something we are given in return. The angels guide our footsteps too, don't forget.

That is another lesson we learn from today's reading: the reality of this spiritual world. How prominent are the angels during this Easter-tide. They guard the tomb; they greet the women with the most wonderful news of Christ's Resurrection, and now they guard over the apostles. They are indeed God's messengers. So it should not be with tongue in cheek that each night we pray for the angels to guard over us during the silent hours of the night as well as during the day. As we grow in our life of freedom in Christ, these beings of the spiritual world will become very real. We are indeed surrounded and protected 'with this great cloud of witnesses' (Heb. 12:1).

This Easter we are being told that nothing must hinder us in our witnessing for Christ by telling of His redeeming, renewing, refreshing life to others as lived out in ours. We are free people walking in the light as all the works of darkness have been dismantled forever at Golgotha.

In Your Resurrection, Lord, You have set me free from all slavery to sin, self and darkness. Now I live in the company of all the angels and saints. Let me respond to Your light and Truth by walking freely and lovingly in Your service. Amen.

Thursday after the Second Sunday of Easter

Obedience to God

*'We gave you explicit orders', he [i.e. the high priest]
said, 'to stop teaching in that name; and what has happened? You have filled Jerusalem with your teaching, . . . '
Peter replied for the apostles: 'We must obey God rather
than men.'*

Acts 5:28-9

Full readings: Acts 5:27-33; Psalm 34:2, 9, 17-20; St. John 3:31-6.

Peter and the apostles had no hesitation in obeying God's command
to preach the good news that eternal life is here, now, in Jesus Christ to
all who repent and seek forgiveness, despite being forbidden to do so
by the religious authorities. As we are seeing in the Easter readings,
the apostles boldly witnessed to the truth of the Risen Jesus who had
been crucified. They were fast realizing that the only true joys to be had
were in fulfilling the will of God, or, as expressed in today's Gospel,
'Whoever puts his faith in the Son has eternal life' (Jn. 3:36). Eternal
life with Jesus was more precious than any worldly treasure, and more
powerful than any order by man. Better to risk bodily punishment and
torture rather than eternal damnation.

What Peter and the apostles teach us was their willingness to
surrender all to God, not only their goods, as we read about a couple of
days ago, but also their wills. They were learning very quickly what
total self-surrender to their Saviour was all about. After all, obedience
to God is the result of self-surrender.

Have we ever seriously contemplated that, when we pray to obey God's will in our lives, what we are in actual fact doing? We are committing a total self-surrender of ourselves to God. This has always been the ultimate aim for all the saints as they strive for that life of complete unity and perfection in Christ. Yet it should not be the goal only for them but for all of us who are baptized into the death of Christ and rise with Him in Paschal glory. By virtue of our baptism we are made saints in the making.

Obedience to God, self-surrender, is our very vocation, just as it was for the members of the Apostolic Church. Thus the prayer 'Lord what will You have me do?' becomes our daily prayer as we surrender our whole being to our God. We are aware we are learning to surrender ourselves to Him when we spend more time thinking about God, and much less on ourselves; when we do not press our own rights or opinions; when we can say willingly at the beginning of each day, 'I commend myself into Your hands, O Lord, do what You will with me.' When we are doing these we are starting to forget ourselves and follow Him.

The Gospel today outlines God sending His Son in this world to bear witness to the Truth so that all who hear and obey Him will have eternal life. But those who do not obey 'the Son will not see that life' (Jn. 3:36). They are unequivocal words. So was Peter's reply to the high priest: 'We must obey God rather than men.'

If we are honest with ourselves, we know during each day there are countless times when we have to choose between God's way and man's way. We realize how many times we opt for the worldly solution and thus disobey God's way. This season of Easter, with its freshness and newness all around us, challenges us to abandon ourselves into the arms of the Risen Lord and to accept His assurance that all things are made new in Him. Indeed, St. Paul reminds us that 'as Christ was raised from the dead by the glorious power of the Father, so also we might set out on a new life' (Rom. 6:4). The glory of Easter is that we are freed from our self-imprisonment through sin. Like the apostles, we become free people content to live for Him in accordance to His will. Like Peter we know 'we must obey God rather than men'. Yet in that surrender is freedom; His service is 'perfect freedom'. But only those who live within His kingdom know and possess this, while millions of others squabble and indeed fight one another for the so-called freedom of possessing. Don't let us be lured from the freedom which Christ's Resurrection gives!

'Lord, what will You have me do?' Direct my footsteps along Your paths, so that I shall always be content to surrender my will in order to obey Yours, and to follow Your precepts in all things. Amen.

Friday after the Second Sunday of Easter

Rejoicing

The apostles went out from the Council rejoicing that they had been found worthy to suffer humiliation for the sake of the name. And every day they went steadily on with their teaching in the temple and in private houses, telling the good news of Jesus the Messiah.

Acts 5:41-2

Full readings: Acts 5:34-42; Psalm 27:1-4, 13-14; St. John 6:1-15.

It is not hard to imagine that the opening verse of today's set psalm would not have been far from the lips of the apostles as they faced and endured the flogging imposed on them by the Council for their continual preaching.

The Lord is my light and my salvation; whom then shall I fear? The Lord is the stronghold of my life; of whom then should I go in dread?

There was absolutely nothing to fear even from a beating because they knew God would give them all the strength they needed in witnessing for Him. Furthermore, they could rejoice in being privileged to suffer for their Saviour. They knew that 'death's mightiest powers have done their worst', and that 'Jesus had his foes dispersed', and they therefore could burst out with 'shouts of praise and joy'.

'Rejoice' and 'again I say rejoice' we sing in the refrain of a well-known hymn by Charles Wesley. Rejoicing these days has tended to be associated with the celebration of some great occasion or event within a family or nation. Yet here, in today's lesson, what a far different reason we discover for a celebration. The apostles were rejoicing in something the world would consider debasing: a flogging. There were no flinchings, no shouts, no shrieking cries of anguish and pain, but patiently enduring it all in the joy of being able to suffer for their Lord. Their joy, their rejoicing, although spontaneous, as all real joy is, is embedded in their longing to serve their Master and spread the wonderful news of this new life in Him. This joy overflows in their fervency to continue their teaching not only in the temple but also in private homes.

We know the rejoicing experienced by the apostles in this situation became the noticeable characteristic of the early Christians. Thus a Christian could easily be discerned in those days simply through his *joie de vivre* in Christ. They preached the *good news* gladly; they suffered torture gleefully; they ran to their martyrs' deaths, thinking it but joy to be able to suffer for Him who had suffered so much for them. The rejoicing of Peter, Paul and Stephen as they were martyred was continued in the lives and martyrdom of such saints as Polycarp of Smyrna and Ignatius of Antioch. The latter begged his fellow Christians not to prevent his being thrown to the wild beasts, as he believed, 'God's wheat I am, and by the teeth of wild beasts I am to be ground that I may prove Christ's pure bread. . . . Then only shall I be a genuine disciple of Jesus Christ when the world will not see even my body.' He passionately wrote:

> May nothing 'seen or unseen', fascinate me, so that I
> may happily make my way to Jesus Christ! Fire, cross,
> struggles with wild beasts, wrenching of bones, mangling
> of limbs, crunching of the whole body, cruel tortures
> inflicted by the devil–let them come upon me, provided
> only I make my way to Jesus Christ.[17]

If these saints were asked why, I am sure they would have answered something like this: 'In what else or who else should we rejoice? In Jesus Christ only is the way, the life and the truth.' As He is also the Living Bread, there is nothing else to hunger after. All their needs were met in and by Him.

As we meditate on the Gospel reading for today, there would have been also much joy and rejoicing by those who followed Jesus to a lonely place in order to learn more of Him. By the shores of Galilee, as the day lengthened and their hunger intensified, Jesus saw their needs, and looked after them by providing bread, ample bread, for them. Joy comes at unexpected moments in very simple occasions and things as we see here. We need to discover that we do not have to wait for what we consider are *the right occasions* for such rejoicing, because THE right occasion is now. It is always upon us as we live in the perpetual Spring of Easter. However, during these great fifty days our rejoicing should be almost tumultuous. That Living Bread is ever within us, and therefore our lives are or should be overflowing with celebration and joy. Of course our Easter hymns are full of these, but some express it more realistically, as in this eighth century hymn of St. John of Damascus:

> The day of Resurrection!
>   Earth, tell it out abroad;
> The Passover of gladness,
>   The Passover of God!
> From death to life eternal,
>   From earth unto the sky,
> Our Christ has brought us over
>   With hymns of victory.
>
> Now let the heavens be joyful,
>   And earth her song begin,
> The round world keep high triumph,
>   And all that is therein;
> Let all things seen and unseen
>   Their notes of gladness blend,
> For Christ the Lord has risen,
>   Our joy that has no end.[18]

One other point before closing: when we can truly rejoice in the Lord, I am sure it helps us to understand more of the suffering, loneliness, unhappiness and dejection of so many people. A Christian is able to do this because rejoicing is a spontaneous act, taking oneself out of oneself. In other words one becomes absorbed in the reason for such joy. For a Christian this is Christ. The more we focus on Christ, the more aware we are of our fellow brothers and sisters. Like the apostles, we want them to share in Christ's healing life too. Two of our daily prayers should be for the healing of Christ's body and unity amongst Christians, and peace within nations, families and individuals. As we give more and more of ourselves to others in our daily living, this too becomes a source for rejoicing.

Your Easter triumph is my rejoicing, dear Lord. Like the apostles and saints of old, let me day by day rejoice in You, and gladly suffer all that life brings, knowing that nothing can take away the reason for my rejoicing–eternal life with You. Amen.

[17] SS. Clement of Rome and Ignatius of Antioch, *The Epistles of St. Clement of Rome and St. Ignatius of Antioch* (The Works of The Fathers, London, 1946), Vol. 1, p.82.

[18] St. John of Damascus, trans. J.M. Neale, in *The New English Hymnal*, Melody edition (Norwich, 1986), pp.178-9.

Saturday after the Second Sunday of Easter

Deacons

The Twelve called the whole company of disciples together and said, 'It would not be fitting for us to neglect
the word of God in order to assist in the distribution.
Therefore, friends, pick seven men of good repute from
your number, men full of the Spirit and of wisdom, and
we will appoint them for this duty.'

Acts 6:2-3

Full readings: Acts 6:1-7; Psalm 33:1-2, 4-5, 18-19; St. John 6:16-21.

Earlier this week we saw how the Apostolic Church lived communally. As membership of this church grew it became impossible for
the Twelve to distribute amongst the very needy, and also to preach the
Word of God. Indeed, today's lesson suggests that the Greek-speaking
widows were already feeling the effect of neglect. To meet this crisis the
Twelve advised the early church to appoint seven men, whom we know
today as deacons, to serve the widows and others in need.

When these seven, Stephen, Philip, Prochorus, Nicanor, Timon,
Parmenas and Nicholas were appointed as fulfilling the conditions of
the Twelve, that is to be 'full of the Spirit and wisdom', the Twelve 'laid
their hands on them', after prayer. Hence we have the beginning of
what became known as three-fold Apostolic ministry of the Church
with this first ordination.

These holy men were ordained deacons to provide a special ministry,
quite distinct from that of the apostles. Theirs was one of serving the

Christian community in what we would call today *works of charity*.[19] St. Ignatius of Antioch wrote of deacons being 'the dispensers of the mysteries of Jesus Christ'. As such they 'should win approval of all in every way; for they are not dispensers of food and drink but ministers of [the] Church of God. Hence they must be on their guard against criticism, as against fire.'[20] By being servants in performing their charitable works, these deacons allowed the apostles to devote all their time to 'prayer and to the ministry of the Word'. Thus, through the combined ministries, the Gospel 'spread more and more widely; [and] the number of disciples in Jerusalem was increasing rapidly' (Acts 6:7).

These deacons were very devout men; Stephen is described as being 'full of grace and power', and so their service to their Christian brethren is the manifestation of their spiritual lives. They reveal how prayer and service are intertwined in our living for Christ. From them we can learn a lot about living out the Gospel. We must spend time in public worship, private prayer and meditation, but it does not stop there if we are to fulfil Our Lord's commandments. One of the good features about the revised Liturgies in Catholic and Anglican churches is that, almost immediately after receiving Our Lord, the Bread of Life, we are dismissed and sent out in to the world. The Liturgy is directing us that once we have received the Blessed Sacrament we must take Christ out with us to do His work in His world. Like the first deacons, our lives must be full of charitable acts for our brothers and sisters. The Jacobean and Caroline divine, Arthur Lake, tells us:

> God who is Charity, gives unto man the gift of charity. But when we have received the gift of God, we must employ it, 'we must not receive the grace of God in vain'. As in nature, so in grace we have our abilities for action, and the parable will tell us what will be our doom, if we hide our talent.

He insists we must not do what 'is contrary unto charity'.[21]

These acts of mercy, as they are also known, begin with those with whom we have the most contact. For most of us that will be members of our families and fellow employees. We must never think that acts of charity are given only to those we hardly know, such as children in an orphanage. Don't forget that an act of charity is something done with love and in Love's name. Members of our own family often need help desperately, but how often do we neglect them? I think one of the saddest things in life is to see a church group raising money for missionary work in some part of the world, when in their midst there are many crying out for love and care. One of our duties as Christians is to become sensitive to the needs of our brothers and sisters living in our neighbourhood. Those 'who are in charity bear one another's burdens and partake each of the other's comforts.'[22]

Lake insists that 'when God says, *you will love*, no man has any excuse to plead, but the malignity of his own nature, yes, no man comes to heaven who did not love.' This means that 'a poor man may love as well as a rich, an ignorant as a wise, [and] a weak as a strong.'[23]

The example of the Apostolic Church illustrated that we must be doing Christians. We shall be judged on how much or how little we have loved. If we want to 'die well and happily' it means that we must 'exercise charity' as much as we are capable of. A near contemporary of Lake, Jeremy Taylor, explained in his *Holy Dying* that as 'religion is the life of the soul' so is 'charity...the life of religion', and 'the great channel through which God passes all His mercy upon mankind.' Taylor believed that 'God cannot...reject a charitable man in his greatest needs and in his most passionate prayers.' After all, 'God Himself is love, and every degree of charity that dwells in us is the participation of the divine nature.'[24]

Charity as performed by the deacons and by the Church ever since has become much maligned. Has this happened because it has no longer been an act of love, but rather a means of relieving one's conscience in respect of the poor and destitute by giving money? This we know is not Christ's meaning of charity, but what man has made it. As Christians we should remember that 'when charity fills the heart of a man, and stretches forth his hand, then he takes a higher place, the place of God, as his ambassador and steward.'[25]

At Easter we are given the greatest gift of all; let us share this in our giving lovingly and caringly to our brothers and sisters.

Like the deacons of the early church I am called to be a servant of

Christ. Help me to meet the spiritual and bodily needs of others by my loving acts and words in Your name. Amen.

[19] Our word deacon comes from the Greek *diakonos*, meaning *servant*.

[20] SS. Clement and Ignatius, op. cit., p.75.

[21] A. Lake, *Sermons with Some Religious and Divine Meditations by Arthur Lake, Bishop of Bath and Wells* (London, 1629), p.289.

[22] Ibid., p.288.

[23] Ibid., p.290.

[24] J. Taylor, *The Whole Works of The Rt. Revd. Jeremy Taylor*, ed. C.P. Eden, 10 vols. (London, 1844-57), Vol. 3, p.302.

[25] A. Farindon, *The Sermons of the Revd. Anthony Farindon, B.D., with his Life*, ed. Thomas Jackson, 4 vols. (London, 1849), Vol. 1, p.432.

The Third Sunday of Easter

Peter

After breakfast Jesus said to Simon Peter, 'Simon son of John, do you love me more than these others?' 'Yes, Lord,' he answered, 'you know that I love you.' 'Then feed my lambs,' He said.

St. John 21:15

Full readings: Acts 5:27-32, 40-1; Psalm 30; Revelations 5:11-14; St. John 21:1-19 (Cycle C).

Peter, emboldened by the Spirit through the Risen Lord, has been the centre of our readings this past week or so. We have seen how Peter is the spokesman for the apostles and the main preacher as he declares the wonders of living in and unto Christ. He has been fearless in challenging the authority of the Jewish religious leaders, and rejoicing in the punishment he and the other disciples have received for their continued inspired preaching and ministry. Through his witnessing to his Risen Lord, the number of Christians grew day by day.

Peter's witnessing was indeed a labour of love. Like St. Mary Magdalen who loved Jesus much because He had forgiven her much, so likewise did Peter. It more than amended for his thrice denial of His Lord. Hence in today's Gospel we see the beginning of this amendment when he thrice affirms to His Master that he did indeed love Him above everything else. It is not hard to imagine that, ever since his denial, foremost in Peter's mind would have been to receive God's forgiveness assuredly. No doubt his daily prayer would have been similar to what

44

we read in today's psalm: 'To you, Lord, I called and pleaded with you for mercy.' Now at last, 'Lord my God, I cried to you and you healed me.' (Ps. 30:2, 8).

Before Jesus confronts Peter, we have a glimpse of the Peter we have been reading about in Acts. Once Peter realized Jesus was standing on the lake shore, and that it was He who had directed them to where they could catch fish, he plunged into the sea and ran the last hundred yards to greet Him. There was no longer any hesitation nor doubt, only spontaneous joy at seeing His Lord, and the delight of being in His presence.

Around the dying fire after the breakfast prepared and blessed by Christ, Peter is truly healed. Our Lord recognized that this disciple had been deeply wounded by his denial. He knew that if Peter was to be the leader of the disciples and to carry on His work, he must firstly be made whole. The thrice repeated 'Do you love me?' is the balm Peter needed, and each time Peter affirmed His love, the balm went further and further into the wounds until all was cleansed. Now cleansed and whole, Peter is equipped to be a true apostle.

What Jesus did for Peter is a lesson for us. We cannot serve Christ faithfully unless we are whole people. If there are grudges, hates, lies, bitterness and jealousies which still possess us, even after many, many years, unless we are prepared to be healed of them and be reconciled to those people involved, we shall never be able to be the person God wants us to be, let alone 'feed [His] Lambs'. Remember the Saviour came to heal all kinds of brokenness:

He has sent me to announce good news to the poor,
To proclaim release for prisoners
and recovery of sight for the blind;
To let the broken victims go free.

(Lk. 4:18)

If any of us still have yokes around our necks, let Christ free us of them; seek forgiveness and let His healing grace penetrate deep within and dissolve every tiny bit of malice, cowardice, hardness and the like. We cannot love if we are still possessed by any of these manifestations of evil. How essential healing is for people to be whole is reflected in the instructions Our Lord gave to His apostles. 'Heal the sick, raise the dead, cleanse lepers, drive out demons' (Mt. 10:8).

The gift of healing from God is such a wonderful thing that we can easily find ourselves proclaiming this goodness in the last two verses of today's psalm.

> You have turned my laments into dancing;
> You have stripped off my sackcloth and clothed me with joy,
> that I may sing psalms to you without ceasing.
> Lord my God, I shall praise you for ever.
>
> (Ps. 30: 11-12)

Let us be like Peter this Eastertide and believe that it is only in the Risen Lord that we can be whole persons. Let us come before Him and seek forgiveness for our sins, the door to healing grace, as we all need this if we are to grow in love. As we continue to read Acts throughout Easter, be mindful how central the healing ministry was in the Apostolic Church, and pray that it is in our Church to-day.

Like Peter, let me embrace You at the dawn of each day, knowing that it is only in You I can be forgiven, cleansed, healed, and restored, from all that is not pure and good. Then I am free for the day to love, praise, thank, and serve You in my daily living and encounters with others. Amen.

Monday after the Third Sunday of Easter

Stephen

Stephen, full of grace and power, began to do great
wonders and signs among the people.... All who were
sitting in the Council fixed their eyes on him, and his face
seemed to them like the face of an angel.

Acts 6:8, 15

Full readings: Acts 6:8-15; Psalm 119:23-30; St. John 6:22-9.

As Stephen had 'chosen the path of faithfulness' (Ps. 119:30), it was
not long before he too drew attention to himself from the religious
fanatics for the 'great wonders and signs' he was doing amongst the
people. Just as many of the Jewish religious leaders wanted Jesus out of
the way, because He challenged them with light and truth to replace the
darkness and falsehood in which they lived, so did Stephen. Evil men
cannot cope with such a challenge as they do not want their very
comfortable existence disturbed. Hence Stephen was arrested and
brought before the authorities just as Our Lord had been.

It was evident even to this Council that the person standing before
them was *special*. Stephen so loved his Lord that this love glowed from
his face. In him there was only goodness, truth and love and this burning desire to be faithful in proclaiming God's work. Tomorrow, when
we read of his martyrdom, this becomes blatantly obvious. It was all
too much for members of the Council when Stephen challenged them
with being 'deaf to the truth', resisting 'the Holy Spirit', murdering 'the

Righteous One' and not keeping the laws given by God. This last accusation particularly stunned his listeners for they prided themselves in keeping the Torah.

Having exposed the truth, Stephen knew there was nothing else he could do for them, and also sensing his imminent death prepared for that moment of glory. As he meditated on such joy, he described his vision of the Son of Man 'standing at the right hand of God'. After such *blasphemy*, the reaction was swift. Dragged to outside the city, Stephen was stoned. However, one really wonders whether in fact Stephen ever felt the impact of those blows, as his spirit had become one with Jesus as he prayed for Him to receive him in His Kingdom. Before dying, like His Master, he must do one thing—plead for this sin not to be held against his executioners. 'Father, forgive them, for they know not what they do.'

Stephen's executioners were people who walked in darkness; they preferred the dark to the light; they had no desire for the Light of Christ to flicker through, let alone penetrate. Such people have no concept of love, and therefore they could not understand nor handle Stephen. However, they do feel the impact of love, but they immediately dismiss it, as they do here with Stephen. The kind of love that radiated from Stephen was cutting and piercing. If it were allowed to cut and pierce they could not abide that as.it would shatter their very foundations.

Unfortunately there are many like those who stoned Stephen in our world today. Like frightened animals they cling to the existence they know. What we have to do as Christians, as Stephen tried to do, is through the power of prayer to make such people aware that Christ's Light and Truth is disturbing, unsettling and terrifying. In piercing, it will tear one's life apart, but it has to be torn apart so it can be rebuilt; rebuilt on love and in truth. That is what the Gospel is all about. That is why Christ came; that is what Stephen preached and why he died, and that is the way people are made whole. In a world where the powers of darkness still do its worst, it is essential that Christians pray daily for Light to alleviate all darkness.

Stephen teaches us we must never be afraid of the truth. He also teaches us we must burn with love for Christ and for every soul on this earth. That means our charity extends to every word and action and thought we have and do. Next time we want to say something unpleasant about another, think of Stephen's purity. Hopefully this will challenge us with thinking something pleasant instead. Our faithfulness must be constant and not fickle. We are faithful not only when it is convenient but when it is most inconvenient, and when it hurts, especially our egos!

Stephen also teaches us how we can live when we have died unto self, when we have emptied ourselves of pride, arrogance, sloth, greed, envy and the like, and replaced it with the gifts of the Spirit. This prayer written by Genesius of Rome (an actor but also a martyr under the Diocletian persecution) could easily have been Stephen's:

> There is but one king I know;
>   It is He whom I love and worship.
> If I were killed a thousand times
>   for my loyalty to Him,
>   I would still be His servant.
> Christ is on my lips.
> Christ is in my heart;
>   no amount of suffering will take Him from me.[26]

This Eastertide let us pray that the Risen Lord will fill us with His gifts of the Spirit such as love, long suffering, meekness and humility, and that 'no amount of suffering will take Him from me'.

My Risen Lord, fill me with Your gifts that I may become like Stephen, so others may know something of Your love by the way I live and the way I speak. Make Your love radiate from my face too. Amen.

---

[26] D. Arnold (ed.), *Praying with the Martyrs* (London, 1991), p.29.

Tuesday after the Third Sunday of Easter

The Bread of Life

Jesus said to them, 'I am the bread of life. Whoever comes to me will never be hungry, and whoever believes in me will never be thirsty.'

St. John 6:35

Full readings: Acts 7:51-8:1; Psalm 31:3-4, 6-8, 17, 21; St. John 6:30-5.

Members of the early church, including Stephen whose martyrdom we read of today, believed with all their being that Jesus is 'the bread of life'. Consequently, if not daily, frequently the early church celebrated the Eucharist. A few years after Stephen, another Christian on his way to martyrdom, Ignatius of Antioch, writing to Christians at Ephesus, spoke of the breaking of 'the same bread' as 'the medicine of immortality, the antidote against death, and the everlasting life in Jesus Christ.'[27] It is not surprising that he advised the early Christians to receive the Bread of Life frequently.[28] Indeed, on his journey to Rome, Ignatius assured members of the Church that he no longer had any 'taste for corruptible food'; his only desire was for 'the Bread of God'... that is, the Flesh of Jesus Christ,... and for my drink I desire His blood, that is, incorruptible love.'[29]

In this discourse Our Lord is emphatic that the bread of which He speaks 'comes down from heaven', that is, the Word incarnate is the eternal bread, because He 'brings life to the world' (Jn. 6:33). Without Him there is no life; we shall always have a hunger and thirst in our lives which will never be fulfilled. That emptiness and gnawing can only be alleviated through Christ, the Bread from heaven.

'I am the Bread of life.' These are very unequivocal words by Jesus, and, although I am not going to suggest that Christians who do not accept the sacraments deny themselves this eternal life of which Jesus speaks, it does seem to me that, if we are striving to live in unison with Christ, this is the main way we do it, by partaking regularly in the Holy Eucharist and receiving Our Lord.

We know that bread is the staff of life, not so much for us who live in the Western world, but it is definitely for those who live in the Middle East. It is also the staff of life for those who travel the world on a shoe-string budget. One can easily survive on ordinary bread and cheese washed down by *vin de pays*, as so many of us know from our own experiences. What Jesus is saying here is that, as we need bread to satisfy our bodily needs, so we need the Heavenly bread to nourish our souls. We should be able to ascertain how frequently our souls need feeding by the frequency with which we eat during the day. We know when we go for long stretches without food how we have a real gnawing feeling, and if we ignore this for too long we become rather faint and weak. We need to eat! The same applies with our souls.

Our Lord is bidding us to come to His banquet; He does not want us to starve ourselves of our spiritual Staff of life. Our Lord, ever patient, ever cajoling, ever beckoning us to come to the Table, is illustrated so well in one of George Herbert's best known poems, *Love bade me welcome*:

> Love bade me welcome: yet my soul drew back,
>   Guilty of dust and sin.
> But quick-eyed Love, observing me grow slack
>   From my first entrance in,
> Drew nearer to me, sweetly questioning,
>   If I lack'd any thing.
>
> A guest, I answer'd, worthy to be here:
>   Love said, You shall be he.
> I the unkind, ungrateful? Ah my dear,
>   I cannot look on Thee.
> Love took my hand, and smiling did reply,
>   Who made the eyes but I?

Truth, Lord, but I have marr'd them: let my shame
  Go where it does deserve.
And know you not, says Love, who bore the blame?
  My dear, then I will serve.
You must sit down, says Love, and taste my meat:
  So I did sit and eat.[30]

The more I meditate on this poem the more I become aware of Jesus being present, as if indeed He is taking my hand, and of experiencing what He meant when He spoke of being the Bread of Life. Make it a favourite of yours, if not already so, and you will discover during this Eastertide another dimension of Love incarnate. It was through Simone Weil's many readings of this poem, that she first encountered Christ, and the essence of prayer. Recitation metamorphosed to prayer.

My blessed Saviour, I know that without Your life I wither and die like the flowers of the field. May I always realize what a precious gift I receive at the altar day by day. As it is so precious, help me never to come without due preparation, but always in penitence for my sins, gratefulness for being part of Your wonderful creation, and in praise thanksgiving for Your precious Life. Amen.

[27] SS. Clement and Ignatius, op. cit., p.68.
[28] Ibid., p.77.
[29] Ibid., p.83.
[30] G. Herbert, *The Works of George Herbert*, 2 vols. (London, 1859), vol. 2, pp.217-8.

Wednesday after the Third Sunday of Easter

Philip

Philip came down to a city in Samaria and began proclaiming the Messiah there. As the crowds heard Philip and saw the signs he performed, everyone paid close attention to what he had to say.

Acts 8:5-6.

Full readings: Acts 8:1-8; Psalm 66:1-7; St. John 6:35-40.

After Stephen was stoned to death, the young Church faced persecution. So severe was this that Christians fled and scattered throughout the region. This in turn enabled the Gospel to be preached to a larger audience. One of those who fled from Jerusalem was Philip, who travelled to Samaria where he proclaimed the coming of the Messiah. His preaching and ministry drew many to experience Christ's healing and presence, and to accept Christ as the Messiah. Indeed, some of the healings were releasing people from being possessed by demons. No wonder Simon thought this magical as the demons were exorcized!

Through his ministry Philip was enabling many to experience what Our Lord is assuring us of in today's gospel. That assurance is that His Father wills that everyone should know and have eternal life. This is given to all who believe in Him, the Son, who will then on the Last Day 'raise them all up' (Jn. 6:39-40).

The Christian life in the way it is meant to be lived out is very simple; this is the way the members of the Apostolic Church knew and taught it. Repent of sin and be baptized. In the waters of Baptism the old

Adam is washed away, and the New is put on: 'we are cleansed from the filth of our sins'.[31] The old way of life has gone, as repentance involves a deliberate turning away from sin and a turning to God.

At this Eastertide when Baptism is part of the Easter Liturgy, it may be helpful three weeks after Easter Day to remind ourselves of the significance of this sacrament. In the words of Origen:

> Let everyone of the faithful recall the words he used in renouncing the devil when first he came to the waters of Baptism, when he took upon himself the first seals of faith and came to the saving fountain; he proclaimed that he would not deal in the pomps of the devil, nor his works, nor would he submit to his servitude and his pleasures.[32]

So animated were the lives of these people, after receiving Baptism from Philip, that a magician, Simon, who lived in the same city and worked *changes* himself through his magic, sought Baptism. Simon is an example to us of all who seek to use God's gifts corruptibly. He wanted the *power* as an end in itself, not as the means to use it in living out Christ's precepts. The very noun *simony* should be a reminder to us all that we should never use Christ's Church to advance ourselves. If we are tempted, let us ponder on this thought: will that give us the eternal life Jesus promised in today's gospel?

Simon was attracted to baptism because he witnessed how powerfully magnetic were the people through whom Christ lives. Baptism made them whole people, and they rejoiced in this. The affirming of our Baptismal vows during the Paschal Liturgy challenges us to ask, have I really turned to Christ? Will others be attracted towards Baptism because of the way I live, or have I abused this sacrament as Simon did?

The Apostolic Church was powerful, yes, but in one way only, in the Spirit of Christ, not in any other way. 'I have no silver or gold; but what I have I give you: in the name of Jesus Christ of Nazareth, get up and walk.' In the name of Christ unclean spirits were driven out; in the name of Christ great and wonderful signs were done amongst the people (Acts 3:6, 5:16, 6:8). Philip in Samaria sought only one thing, to obey his Lord's command to preach the gospel, heal the sick and comfort those in need, so that people could know the means of having eternal life in Christ. This Eastertide let us strive to be more like Philip and less like Simon.

As I renew my Baptismal vows this Eastertide, may they remind me of what is meant by being a Christian. It is one who dies daily unto sin, to the standards of this world and any kind of self-seeking. In rising with You, O Christ, from the waters of Baptism, You have made me Yours, not only your sister or brother but heiress or heir to an incorruptible and eternal kingdom. Give me grace to follow Your way so I may live within Your kingdom. Amen.

[31] H. Bettensen, *Early Fathers*, p.180.
[32] Ibid., p.246.

Thursday after the Third Sunday of Easter

The Ethiopian

As they were going along the road, they came to some water. 'Look,' said the eunuch, 'here is water: what is to prevent my being baptized?'...Then they both went down into the water, Philip and the eunuch, and he baptized him.

Acts 8:36, 38

Full readings: Acts 8:26-40; Psalm 66:8-9, 16-17, 20; St. John 6:44-51.

Setting out once again from Jerusalem, Philip journeyed from Caesarea on a desert road towards Gaza. Along the way he meets an Ethiopian returning home after making a pilgrimage to Jerusalem. As the Ethiopian rests awhile from his travelling, he reads part of the Scriptures. What he reads is significant as this is the very good news that the disciples were preaching about. Although he does not understand to whom Isaiah is referring as the lamb being led to the slaughter, Philip, who has been prompted by the Spirit to join him, does. As Philip explains that the lamb is Jesus who has lately been crucified, but raised up by God, the Ethiopian is greatly moved. Undoubtedly he desired this new life in Christ with all his heart, so much so that when they came to the first pool of water, the eunuch sought baptism there and then. 'What is to prevent my being baptized?' There was absolutely nothing as he believed in Jesus and desired to live in the new life in Him. The water of baptism liberated him from all his past sin. Out in the desert, under the soaring sun, he was born anew.

Life would never be the same again as he continued his journey homeward bound. Perhaps lines similar to the opening verses from today's psalm would not have been far from his lips:

Let all the earth acclaim God.
Sing to the glory of His name,
make His praise glorious.

I imagine we can say without too much exaggeration that our Ethiopian, in the imagery used by St. Ignatius of Antioch, became a stone 'of the Father's temple, prepared for the edifice of God the Father, to be taken aloft by the hoisting engine of Jesus Christ, that is, the cross, while the Holy Spirit serves you as a rope.' Undoubtedly, like Ignatius, he would also confess that 'faith is your spiritual windlass' and love is the 'road which leads us to God.'[33]

The Ethiopian eunuch went on his way rejoicing. How often do we discover that to know Jesus is a matter of rejoicing? Philip had left this man immediately after baptizing him. Yet this does not perturb him because through Philip's hands he has been given all that he needs, this new life in Jesus Christ. He discovered what it means to be an Easter person. The great Fifty Days is a time of much rejoicing, or should be, because like the eunuch we have been assured of this new life in the Risen Christ. In fact, our rejoicing should not cease at Pentecost! Our lives should ooze with joy and gladness every day, but do they? Sometimes we act as the most miserable creatures out, as if we have been condemned to a life of darkness and despair. How contrary this is to what Jesus has been assuring us in the gospel readings this week. What more could we want or desire than the gift of eternal life? This is the gift Christ offers each one of us at Easter. When we let ourselves dwell too much on the darker aspects of life, I am sure this hymn of praise by Hippolytus of Rome will redirect our thoughts, upwards.

Christ is risen:
The world below lies desolate.
Christ is risen:
The spirits of evil are fallen.
Christ is risen:
The angels of God are rejoicing.

Christ is risen:
    The tombs of the dead are empty.
Christ is risen indeed from the dead,
    The first of the sleepers.
Glory and power are his forever and ever.
                                Amen.[34]

Thank you, O blessed Lord, for Your risen life which gives me eternal life. May I rejoice daily for what this has given me: freedom, hope, fearlessness, and that desire to love and serve You forever. Amen.

[33] SS. Clement and Ignatius, op. cit., pp.63-4.
[34] Arnold, op. cit., p.10.

Friday after the Third Sunday of Easter

Conversion – Saul becomes Paul

'Saul, Saul, why are you persecuting me?'
'Tell me, Lord,' he said, 'who you are?'
The voice answered, 'I am Jesus, whom you are persecuting. But now get up and go into the city, and you will be told what you have to do.'

Acts 9:4-6

Full readings: Acts 9:1-20; Psalm 117; St. John 6:52-9.

If we ever need any proof that the Easter message is true I don't think we have to look any further than Paul's experience along the Damascus road. Here was a man whose whole being was dedicated to the persecution of Christians, and so fanatic was he in this, that he deliberately sought permission from the religious authorities to hound them like dangerous animals that needed to be caught and killed to safeguard people's lives. What happens? Our Lord intervenes! Jesus stands before him. Saul is confronted with the Light, and so piercing is this light that he is blinded. No longer can any of his darkness be hidden. Every facet of his whole existence up to that point is challenged by Truth and Light as his soul is gradually cleansed in order to be filled with Life, life of the Risen Christ.

Jesus gives him space before making him a fully-fledged Christian. Those three days which Saul was given in complete darkness must have been three of the most enlightening but painful days of his life. Everything that was not fit to be Paul had to be let go; he had to find the person God had made.

> 'Lord, You have examined me and You know me. . . . For
> there is not a word that I speak but You, Lord, know
> all about it. . . . Where can I escape from Your spirit,
> where from Your presence? . . . You know me through
> and through.'
>
> (Ps. 139 *passim*)

While Saul is preparing himself for the next direction from Christ, Ananias, already a devout Christian, also has a vision of Jesus. He is directed to restore Saul's sight. So widespread had Saul's persecution of the Church become known, that Ananias at first is very reluctant to do as commanded, until assured by his Lord that he must because He had chosen Saul to do His work. In the house on Straight Street, Damascus, through the laying on of hands by Ananias, Saul receives the gift of the Holy Spirit. Healing and thus transformation is swift in his case. He is baptized and immediately he sets out to preach Jesus, but not before he had eaten after his three days of fasting.

What happened in Paul's life is indicative of what can happen in anybody's life, once Jesus has penetrated. Perhaps the circumstances may not be as powerful and overwhelming as those experienced by Saul but the change can be just as real. The passion Saul possessed in persecuting Christians was automatically transferred to his preaching Jesus Christ and labouring in His Church with the same intensity. Our friends and families should be just as astounded at our change as the people in Damascus were of Paul's. Becoming a Christian is being a new person. As this new person each of us grows in grace, and as we grow in grace we are made more aware of the vastness of God's goodness within us and His kingdom and the many gifts we receive as subjects of that kingdom.

If there is not a newness, a freshness or growing in our lives, we have to ask ourselves why. Is it that we accept the Word of God formally, but never put it into action? Are we still living in a two-storeyed house, where on the first floor we deal with those things we consult God about, and on the second floor we deal with those matters which we place outside His will?

Just as Christ needed Paul to do His work in the first century, so He needs us today, perhaps even more so. He needs Christian men and women filled with the Spirit and fervently manifesting Jesus Christ. With so much brokenness, hatred, violence and injustice in our world, we must do all we can to alleviate this. The truth of the Lord does endure for ever, but He needs us to proclaim it.

During this Easter season we are constantly being reminded of newness, of life, the new life in Christ. Perhaps we hear it so often that we tend to forget that newness only comes from something which hitherto has died or been dormant. This is the Spring in our lives, and we know that Spring is the most beautiful time of the year. However, for Christians Spring is every day. To live in Christ means we have to die unto self not once, but many times each day. Every time we say 'yes' to Him, not only do we become a little stronger within ourselves, but we strengthen the whole Christian community and make it more beautiful. This Eastertide and always let our lives be like the first leaves and the first shoots of Spring.

Dear Saviour, I need to be constantly shaken by Your Holy Spirit so that I do not lapse into periods of dying or stagnating in my witness to You. Make my whole being burn with a passionate desire to live and serve You only each day, so that my being glows with Your beauty. Amen.

Saturday after the Third Sunday of Easter

Tabitha

In Joppa there was a disciple named Tabitha who filled her
days with acts of kindness and charity. At that time she fell
ill and died. . . . Peter . . . knelt down and prayed; then turning towards the body, he said, 'Tabitha, get up.' She opened
her eyes, saw Peter and sat up.

Acts 9:36-7,40

Full readings: Acts 9:31-42; Psalm 116:12-17; St. John 6:60-9.

In today's lesson we have a glimpse of the early Church in action
during a period of peace and solidarity. There were indeed some
remarkable women and men who were living in close-knit Christian
communities 'in the fear of the Lord'. One of these was in Joppa where
Tabitha and many other women spent their time in prayer and acts of
charity. When Tabitha died, perhaps unexpectedly, the depth of their
belief in Jesus and faith in prayer were illustrated when they immediately sent for Peter in nearby Lydda. Peter, who had been healing
the sick there, came quickly, and after kneeling in prayer he commanded Tabitha to 'get up'. Tabitha's raising from the dead manifests
how receptive Peter and the disciples were to the Spirit who gives life.
Amazing healings had been taking place, and Tabitha's raising is the
climax of Peter's healings as recorded in Acts.

This healing ministry through Peter's life shows he is at one with His
master now. Like Paul, his life is the living out of Easter. Their

unequivocal witness to Christ is even more evident in the juxtaposition-
ing of the lesson with the gospel for today. Here, instead of more and
more being added to the numbers following Christ, they diminished as
Our Lord's teaching became either too unacceptable or difficult for
them. In the midst of all this it is Peter who acknowledges, when Jesus
challenged the Twelve about also leaving, that there is no point in
leaving and going elsewhere. As *shaky* as his faith was at that stage, he
nevertheless recognized that it is only in Jesus that there is life. 'Lord,
to whom shall we go? Your words are words of eternal life. We believe
and know that you are God's Holy One.' (Jn. 6:68-9) Peter believed
that Jesus is the Word of God, the giver of all life. Now in the early
Church his life is a living witness to this. He is Christ's instrument of
bringing eternal life to all who believe; he continues Christ's ministry of
healing all manner of disease, paralysis and now death itself. The
raising of Tabitha through Peter's prayers and ministry, coming after his
many healings, is not unlike the timing of Jesus' raising of Lazarus in
the gospel.

We have been reading this past week that there were many 'wonders
and signs' done amongst the people. One of the lessons we learn from
re-reading Acts this Easter is what is accomplished by the Church when
it is unified in prayer and acts of charity towards each other. Christ is a
powerful force working through the members of the various Christian
communities. We can indeed learn a lot from Luke's account of the
Apostolic Church and from the writings of the saints who lived shortly
afterwards. Ignatius of Antioch stressed how 'devoted' he was 'to
unity', and exhorted his fellow Christians 'never to act in a spirit of
factiousness, but according to what you have learnt in the school of
Christ.' He assured them 'where there is division and passion, there is
no place for God.' For Ignatius 'the official record is Jesus Christ; the
inviolable record is His Cross and His death and His Resurrection, and
the faith of which He is the Author.'[35]

Of course there were dissensions. We have only to read Paul's letters to the Corinthians to realise that, and a few years later St. Clement
of Rome also upbraided them for their 'division and wrath', when he
wrote:

> Why are quarrels and outbursts of passion and divi-
> sions and war in your midst? Or, do we not have one God

and one Christ and one Spirit of grace, a Spirit that was poured out upon us? And is there not one calling in Christ? Why do we tear apart and disjoint the members of Christ and revolt against our own body, and go to such extremes of madness as to forget that we are mutually dependent members?

Their schism had indeed 'perverted many' and caused 'discouragement'; it had also 'bewildered' many, 'and to all of us it has brought sorrow'. All of this is thus 'exceedingly disgraceful and unworthy of your training in Christ,' he reprimanded. He therefore implored them to love one another in Christ. It is 'love [which] unites us to God'; it is 'love [which] endures everything, is long-suffering to the last; . . . love creates no schism; love preserves perfect harmony.'[36]

What St. Clement told the Corinthian Church is a sober warning to us who are so often divided, even to the point of hatred. We must keep Christ's command 'to love one another' constantly in our very being. St. Clement's petition on peace and unity is also worth reflecting on this Eastertide:

> Grant concord and peace to us as well as to all the inhabitants of the earth, just as You did grant it to our fathers, when they piously 'called upon You in faith and truth', grant us to be obedient to Your almighty and glorious name, as well as to our princes and rulers on earth.[37]

Dear Lord, You died and rose again for all of us; and therefore in You we are united as Your brothers and sisters, give me a sense of urgency in praying and working towards the unity of Your Body in this world, still so torn asunder. May my prayer help towards that day when we all shall be one with You at the altar, receiving the Bread of Life from the same hands. Amen.

[35] SS. Clement and Ignatius, op. cit., p.88.
[36] Ibid., pp.37-9.
[37] Ibid., p.47.

The Fourth Sunday of Easter

The Good Shepherd

The Lord is my shepherd; I lack for nothing.
He makes me lie down in green pastures,
He leads me to water where I may rest;
He revives my spirit.

Psalm 23:1-3

Full readings: Acts 2:14, 36-41; Psalm 23; 1 Peter 2:20-5; St. John 10:1-10.

One of the most comforting images for us Christians is Christ as the Good Shepherd, because we know a shepherd always takes care of his sheep and protects them from all dangers, or put in the words of the most popular psalm, 'The Lord is my shepherd; there is nothing I shall want', and I shall 'fear no harm'. The Shepherd is the door! Thus nothing can enter without His knowing–no thieves nor robbers, and so all within the fold are safe.

Not only does the shepherd protect but he leads. He leads his flock to water and pastures. The Shepherd is continually leading us to His Heavenly Banquet to be fed and refreshed. Unlike the shepherd who sometimes has difficulty in finding fresh water and pasture for his sheep, we under our Shepherd never experience any lack of refreshments. We are replenished every day.

It is only those who refuse to be led by the Shepherd who go hungry and thirsty. In our reading from Acts we have seen how the Jews decided they would prefer to live without nourishment at the hands of the Shepherd. However, what they refused was embraced by the Gentiles with open arms. Jesus wants to be the good Shepherd to all. He died and rose for all, both Jew and Gentile, but He does not force Himself nor His Risen life on any. He is only the Bread and Water of Life for those who come in search of it, that is, those who 'acknowledge that the Lord is God [who] made us and we are His. His own people, the flock which He shepherds' (Ps. 100:3).

At the Easter Vigil we affirmed our Baptismal promises, and therefore assented to being a member of Christ's flock. As a member of His flock we should be content to be guided; we thus have no wish to venture outside because we know that our Shepherd has 'the words of eternal life'. After all, there is nowhere else to go! If perchance we do wander from the flock, what then? We know from Our Lord's teaching that the shepherd will always make every effort to find the lost sheep. Christ searches and searches for us in the anticipation that He will find our hearts. What we have to ask ourselves on this Good Shepherd Sunday, if by chance we have strayed from the fold of Christ, is whether we are prepared to let Christ find us and bring us back within His arms and be tenderly let down in His fold? This Sunday's readings are commending that such is Christ's love for us that He desperately wants all of us to be led by Him and shelter under His protection. This is brought out in these few lines by Richard Crashaw.

> Live, O for ever live and reign
> The Lamb who his own love hath slain!
> And let Thy lost sheep live to inherit
> That Kingdom which this Cross did merit.[38]

Of course, as we live out the Christian life we know only too well that we do have to face the dangers from preying wolves. To be a true witness to Christ, our Good Shepherd, it means we do have to leave the enclosure time and time again. Just as Jesus came to seek the *lost sheep*, so must we as we must always remember that Christ has no other hands or feet in this world now but ours. That has been His commission to us because He needs us to continue the shepherding. We must care for others with the same tenderness and compassion as He would. Being a shepherd for Christ means we have to be prepared to get ourselves dirty, dishevelled and disarrayed as we seek the *lost*. Love as exemplified by the Good Shepherd always means going out of our way, it always means it must cost us something of ourselves all the time. However, the wonderful thing about this Christian life is that when we have spent ourselves we always have the means for refuelling and recharging in order to be spent over and over again. Our lives will be a succession of 'going out and coming in' as Christ knows His sheep.

> Christ who knows all His sheep
> Will all in safety keep;
> He will not lose his blood,
>   Nor intercession:
> Nor we the purchased good
>   Of His dear Passion.[39]

So on this Good Shepherd Sunday let yourself be nourished by the Food the Shepherd gives within His fold, so in turn you may go out from it to bring sustenance to the hungry, drink for the thirsty, shelter for the homeless, comfort to the dying and lonely and hope to all.

Thank You, dear Lord, for being a Shepherd to me. I know as such You will always provide my every want and care for me, and even come looking for me when I stray to bring me home on Your shoulder. In gratitude for Your goodness to me, teach me in turn to be a true shepherd to all I meet. Amen.

[38] R. Crashaw, *Crashaw's Poetical Works*, ed. I.C. Martin (Oxford, 1927), p.279.
[39] Richard Baxter, *The Good Shepherd*, in *The English Poets*, ed. R. Etchells (London, 1990), p.76.

Monday after the Fourth Sunday of Easter

Universalism

> News came to the apostles and members of the church
> in Judaea that Gentiles too had accepted the word of
> God....
> God gave them no less a gift than He gave us when we
> came to believe in the Lord Jesus Christ.
>
> Acts 11:1, 17

Full readings: Acts 11:1-18; Psalm 42:2-3, 43:3-4; St. John 10:11-18.

Today within the Church we accept very easily that Christ died and
rose from death for everyone, before His time and after. However, in
the Apostolic Church this at first was not accepted, and when Gentiles
were first admitted into the Church it threatened to divide the Church
which at that time was mainly Jewish. Even Peter as a Jew did not wish
to preach to, and baptize the non-Jew until the Holy Spirit commanded
him.

Thus the lesson for today describes how Peter was alerted to preach
the Gospel 'to all nations' when he was staying at Joppa after having
raised Tabitha to life. In a vision he is directed by God that all things
created by Him are clean; nothing is profane. While he is pondering on
the meaning of his apparition, he receives a message that Cornelius, a
Gentile, awaits him, seeking the Holy Spirit. At once the significance of
his vision was apparent. 'I now understand how true it is that God has
no favourites, but that in every nation those who are godfearing and do
what is right are acceptable to Him.' (Acts 10:34-5).

However, when Peter returned to Jerusalem the Christian Jews there 'took issue with him'. To assure them that God meant the Gospel to be preached to the non-Jews, Peter had to relate his vision, and tell how this coincided with the arrival of Cornelius from Caesarea. 'How could I stand in God's way?' (Acts 11:17). With such forthrightness from Peter, his Jewish friends were persuaded 'that God has granted life-giving repentance to the Gentiles also.' (Acts 11:18).

Peter's experience is a very sobering lesson for us. So often we want to be insular about our faith. However, there can never be anything insular about being a Christian. It is something which must always be shared within our community. The promise of eternal life is *common*; it is offered to all, irrespective of wealth and high-ranking position or poverty and servitude. It is only through Christ that all classes and races can embrace because all are classless and raceless in Him. If only this concept would take root within us, then so many of this world's hatreds would disappear!

Universalism is the clear message of Christ's command before His ascension. He distinctly commissioned His apostles to go out 'to all nations and make them My disciples; baptize them in the name of the Father and the Son and the Holy Spirit, and teach them to observe all that I have commanded you.' (Mt. 28:19-20). The history of the Western and Eastern churches manifests how the early Christians, despite death, persecution and all kinds of hardships, took this command seriously. Through them and generations of Christians after them, the fruits of the Gospel have been sown in every corner of this globe.

Through their efforts we still possess the rudiments of the Christian faith, but our country is no longer Christian. We are now living in a post-Christian era. England and other western countries need to be reconverted to the Christian faith. Therefore the same urgency is needed today as it was in the Apostolic Church. Just as Peter was led by the Spirit to preach the Good News to all, so are we today. If this world is ever to embrace Christ again, then we must allow ourselves to be filled and led by the Spirit so we can preach the Gospel, not so much by words but by actions, where we live and work. It is only by living a Christ-like life that others will notice how different our lives are from those who live *good* lives, and there are many who do. In fact, many live better in this sense of goodness than do many of us practising Christians. However, this world, so torn by violence, hatred, apathy, greed and lust, desperately needs to hear the news of a Saviour, of One who has overcome all of these and who gives new life, and a purpose for living. Sheer good living won't do this. Let us be generous in sharing the Easter message with others. It is only through the Spirit of Christ that Truth and Light can prevail. It is only these which scatter deceit and darkness. 'O Christ, [You are] the loveliest Light that ever shone.'[40]

O my Risen and glorified Lord, Your arms stretched forth on the Cross to embrace all mankind, give me Your grace to be a worthy disciple and to live out Your command of manifesting the Gospel wherever I am and in whatever I am doing. Amen.

[40] C. Rossetti, *The Poetical Works of Christina Georgina Rossetti, with Memoir and Notes by W.M. Rossetti (London, 1904), p.269.*

Tuesday after the Fourth Sunday of Easter

Christian Fellowship

For a whole year the two of them lived in fellowship with the church there, and gave instruction to large numbers. It was in Antioch that the disciples first got the name of Christians.

Acts 11:26

Full readings: Acts 11:19-26; Psalm 87:1-7; St. John 10:22-30.

It is not without significance that it is at Antioch that the followers of Christ were first called Christians. The Apostolic Church in Antioch I have always imagined to be as close to the ideal of Christian living as possible. Luke certainly gives this impression as he describes the activities of the Christians there. When Barnabas arrived in Antioch he already found 'the divine grace at work', implying that both Jew and Gentile Christians were living out the Gospel. After the persecution which followed Stephen's martyrdom, the early Christians had scattered throughout the region. Some of these had come to Antioch. As these included both Jew and Gentile Christians, it meant that the Gospel was preached without excluding anyone.

When Barnabas arrived he immediately gave his support to the Church by rejoicing in their Christ-like living, and encouraging them to be steadfast in the faith. To help him in his ministry to the Christians at Antioch, he sought out Paul in nearby Tarsus. Together, we are told, they lived within the fellowship of the Church there in Antioch, and instructed them in the Christian faith.

So often we Christians of the twentieth century forget that the essence of belonging to Christ's Church is the fellowship which results from it. Every local church is a community in which we share all that we have and are with the other members. By fellowship we do not mean simply enjoying the social activities and having a good time. These are indeed part, but only a part. We also must share our offering up the Eucharist, our prayers, our talents, our listening, our caring, and our growing in the Christian life. We must share our spiritual experiences of the Faith, and not be shy about speaking of the things of God. We should be able to talk about aspects of the Kingdom of God as easily as about the weather.

Barnabas was not only 'a good man', but a man 'full of the Holy Spirit and of faith'. Indeed, it can rightly be said that his goodness is the result of the Holy Spirit living within him. His life amongst the Christians at Antioch teaches us that if we are going to be lively and effective members of our Christian community we too must be 'full of the Holy Spirit and of faith'.

One of the characteristics of a real Christian community is harmony and common assent, where the numbers increase daily. This is precisely what happened in Antioch; 'large numbers were won over to the Lord'. If this is not happening within our parish, perhaps we should ask ourselves are we truly being Easter people? Is the risen and glorified Lord transforming our lives? Do we want others to share in this newness of life? Could we be called Christians simply through the way we live, as the disciples were in Antioch? The church in Antioch certainly challenges us to reassess our lives as Christians.

If we read to the end of chapter eleven, we shall discover that the church in Antioch did not live simply for its own members. It was not introspective at all, and its members enthusiastically saw themselves as part of the wider Christian community. They were ready to support their fellow Christians elsewhere. Aware that famine was occurring in Judaea, they all gave according to their means to relieve the plight of the Christians there. We too have to be just as enthusiastically aware of the wider community. Of course, we still see today glimpses of sharing when some major catastrophe hits some part of the world. However, it is the ever-continuing plights in our midst that are often overlooked and that we need to support, such as the homeless. These are our brothers and sisters in Christ. Barnabas and Paul would not have overlooked them. Neither should we. Let us too be 'a good man' or woman, 'full of the Holy Spirit and of faith'.

I thank You, O most holy and blessed Trinity, that I have been made a member of Your Church through my Baptism. Help me to be a responsible member of my Christian community by sharing and giving of all I have, but also to be aware of the needs of the universal church. Amen.

Wednesday after the Fourth Sunday of Easter

The First Missionary Journey

While they were offering worship to the Lord and fasting, the Holy Spirit said, 'Set Barnabas and Saul apart for me, to do the work to which I have called them.' Then, after further fasting and prayer, they laid their hands on them and sent them on their way.

Acts 13:2-3

Full readings: Acts 12:24–13:5; Psalm 67:2-3, 5-6; St. John 12:44-50.

Yesterday I wrote about the early church in Antioch, and finished with its outreaching to Christians facing famine in Judaea. In today's lesson that outreaching continues, but in a different strand. This time it is towards those who are not Christian. I noted yesterday how close this Church came to the ideal, and today we are given another opportunity to see why in Antioch the disciples were first called Christians. During their times of worship and fasting together it became obvious to them that the Holy Spirit was directing them to send two of their teachers, Barnabas and Paul, further afield to do the Lord's work.

This commissioning of Barnabas and Paul by the church at Antioch led to what is known as the first missionary journey. It was a journey which would take them across the sea to Cyprus and then across to the Asia Minor coast. It was also a journey which brought much physical pain and torture, but for Paul it became a prelude to a life of suffering in Christ's name, when they met with so much opposition from the Jews either resident in the town where they were preaching, or from nearby, who came to stir up trouble.

In view of the response of the Jews to the teaching of the Good News by Barnabas and Paul as they travelled from town to town, today's Gospel reading is an apt reminder of what happens to those who choose to stay in darkness rather than live in the light. For those who reject the light of Christ have already brought judgment upon themselves. Christ's words are worth reflecting on for a moment. 'There is a judge for anyone who rejects me and does not accept my words; the word I have spoken will be his judge on the last day.' (Jn. 12:48). This means we shall be judged according to what Jesus has taught us.

The purpose of Christ's teaching and those who follow His command to preach the Word is to bring people out of darkness into His marvellous light. To those who responded to Barnabas and Paul's preaching, and believed in Christ, there was deliverance from such darkness. In Christ they entered 'eternal life'. This entering eternal life is at the heart of the Resurrection teaching. The whole symbolism of the Easter Vigil is that we pass from darkness into light. As the Paschal candle is lit these words are said: 'May the light of Christ, rising in glory, dispel the darkness of our hearts and minds.' The splendour of this light is captured in John Keble's translation of one of the oldest hymns in Christendom, the Greek *Phos hilaron*:

> O gladsome light, O grace
> O God the Father's face,
> The eternal splendour wearing;
> Celestial, holy, blest,
> Our Saviour Jesus Christ
> Joyful in Your appearing.[41]

Another part of the Easter Vigil service where this comparison between darkness and light is made is in the Baptism. However, in our liturgy much of the symbolism that was in the early Church has been lost. There in the semi-darkness the candidates faced west to renounce the devil and all works of darkness, after which they turned towards the east as they ascended from the font to announce their belief in Christ. Still facing east they were handed a lighted candle, symbolizing that from now onwards they were children of the light. St. Francis of Assisi in one of his canticles conveyed this transition:

In Christ I'm newly born again:-
The old man dead, the new restored;
And whilst my heart is cleft in twain,
Transferred by love as by a sword,
My Spirit, all on fire, would fain
Behold the beauty of its Lord.[42]

Hence this newness of life, which is given through Christ's Resurrection, begins at our Baptism and lasts for ever. We are raised with Christ to eternal life, and thus walk with Christ in light. So this Easter we are called once again not to let that light hide behind a bushel, but to let it shine to glorify God, and like Paul and Barnabas use it to show others to Christ.

O Risen Saviour, may I continually affirm my Baptismal vows so that I may always walk in the light. Whenever I succumb to any works of darkness, let me be swift to disown it, so that I may not hinder Your grace working within me. Amen.

[41] John Keble in *The New English Hymnal*, op. cit., p.375.
[42] St. Francis of Assisi, *The Works of. . . St. Francis of Assisi*, trans. by a religious of that order (London, 1882), p.156.

Thursday after the Fourth Sunday of Easter

Servants

In very truth I tell you, a servant is not greater than his master, nor a messenger than the one who sent him.

St. John 13:16

Full readings: Acts 13:13-25; Psalm 89:2-3, 21-2, 25, 27; St. John 13:16-20.

We all know that a servant is one who serves, that is, waits on implementing the will and demands of another. The supreme example of servitude is in Christ who waited on His Father, and lived according to His will, even when fulfilling that will meant drinking the cup of bitter wine in the garden of Gethesemane. On that same night before entering the garden, Our Lord, after doing the servant's job of washing the disciples' feet, commanded them in turn to be servants in His world. In today's lesson, as we follow Barnabas and Paul on this first missionary journey, we are conscious that they are carrying out Our Lord's command to be servants, not only servants to their fellow human beings, but especially to their Master.

They gladly preached the Gospel wherever they journeyed. In today's reading we find them preaching in Antioch in Pisidia. Here they explained how Jesus was the fulfilment of all the signs God had shown the Jewish nation, His chosen race.

In teaching about the position of a servant, Jesus had instructed His apostles that 'a servant is not greater than his master' (Jn. 15:20). So, if the Master is persecuted, so will be his servants. Barnabas and

Paul were to discover how true this was before their journey ended. Nevertheless, they counted it joy to suffer expulsion, stoning and beating for their Lord.

To be a servant one has to be humble. This is one of the main lessons Christ taught us by His life. He was content to wash feet; He gladly let His back be lashed; He welcomed the company of the outcast; He enjoyed a meal with a publican. Yet we find it very hard at times to follow Our Lord's examples. If we are scrupulously honest we would find doing these things rather demeaning. However, until we can undertake such tasks gladly for Our Lord we shall never taste the kingdom of heaven. As long as we always want to feel superior, proud, and in command of every situation then we shall never know Christ. We shall never discover the real meaning of His teaching nor the purpose of His life and His promise of the Spirit. We always have to realize we have a choice of being a servant to Christ in this world or a slave to our whims and wants. We can only be faithful to one master!

If there is difficulty in deciding which master to follow, we should understand that being a servant to one leads to freedom, and to the other servitude. The Easter message makes it rather obvious which brings freedom. It is only in Him who has triumphed over the servitude of sin in all its various forms—greed, lust, envy, hatred, malice and revenge—who can deliver us from them. So if you find it difficult to be humble and lowly, know that it can become part of your life by allowing the Risen Christ to take possession of it. It is only in Him that we can learn to be humble and grow in humility and in likeness to Him. There is not any other way, and the way to experience the Risen Christ is always via Calvary. Humility is not a virtue of this world, it will always be costly in terms of this world; but in terms of the heavenly kingdom it is a pearl of great price. Archbishop Fenelon reminds us that 'humility is the foundation stone of all graces and holiness; it is so delicate and sensitive a virtue that, as we speak about it or as we seek to find it, we can make it wither.' So often we have a false notion of what is humility. Fenelon showed clearly the distinction between 'false humility' and 'true humility'. He believed people had 'false humility' when they believed themselves 'unworthy of God's goodness and [dare] not look to it with trust.' On the other hand, 'true humility [means]...seeing one's own unworthiness, and giving one's self up to God, never doubting that He can work out the greatest results for and in us.'[43] It may also be helpful to realise that the word *humility* comes from the

Latin *humus* meaning the earth or ground. We know that our earth is the servant of mankind, often abused by the way it is used, and mostly taken for granted. When we are truly humble, we allow ourselves to be used like the earth and absorb all the refuse within us lovingly, and the many, many times we are taken for granted by others. In doing so, we know that we shall never be taken for granted by the One with whom it matters. Just as the earth responds to warmth and moisture, despite all its tramplings, and brings forth her fruits, so our souls will harvest from our humility. Let us therefore this Paschaltide decide we truly want to be like Barnabas and Paul and be Christ's servant whatever the cost involved in being truly humble.

O my blessed Lord, You became a servant in order to give me life eternal: give me Your grace to be a faithful servant to You by living humbly each day. Let me glory in any kind of misunderstanding and hardship for You. Amen.

[43] F. Fenelon, *The Spiritual Letters of Archbishop Fenelon: Letters to Women*, trans. H.L.S. Lear (London, 1877), p.36.

Friday after the Fourth Sunday of Easter

The Way

And if I go and prepare a place for you, I shall come again and take you to Myself, so that where I am you may be also; and you know the way I am taking.

St. John 14:3-4

Full readings: Acts 13:26-33; Psalm 2:6-11; St. John 14:1-6.

In His farewell discourses Jesus wanted to assure His disciples that all would be well despite what the world would endeavour to do to Him. One of these assurances was that He would prepare a place for them in His native land. Another was that by being with Him these last three years, they knew or should know the way to it. For Thomas it was the latter. He always had to have everything spelled out. So he blurted out, 'Lord, we do not know where You are going, so how can we know the way?' (Jn. 14:5). To this, Jesus answers very plainly, 'I am the way, the truth, and the life; no one comes to the Father except by me' (Jn. 14:6).

We know from the Easter narratives that Thomas did not understand Our Lord's reply to him. He was still looking for an anchor after the Resurrection. It was not until he felt the wounds of Christ that Thomas comprehended Christ in the way that Christ had taught of Himself.

Have we fully accepted Christ as the way, the only way? It is the only way which leads to everlasting life. Through Him is the only way to experience life in all its fullness and richness. Yet we always have to remember that, rich as life is in Christ, it is only experienced by the way of the Cross. The Resurrection can never be separated from the Crucifixion. Lancelot Andrewes expresses this togetherness like this: 'Christ's dying, and His rising are so linked together, and their audits so entangle one with another, as it is very hard to sever them.'[44] In his 1623 Paschal sermon, through wine-press imagery, where Christ is both pressed and the presser, he conveys this unity. At the pressing of grapes flows red wine, symbolic of the Christ's blood which gushed out after His trampling upon at Gabbatha and Golgotha. This blood in turn symbolized 'the cup of salvation'. On Easter Day, now clothed in white, He is the wine presser as He has crushed all satanic power.[45]

So 'Christ is our way', leading us surely 'in His laws. And in His Body mightily bears us up to heaven.'[46] Thus, in knowing the way which leads to our home prepared by the Risen Lord, we realize it is not going to be a straight and easy road. Barnabas and Paul discovered this in their missionary endeavours in Asia Minor, as have so many of the saints since then.

We shall know we are walking the way if it costs us something. Following Christ to our eternal home will inevitably be a costly experience in terms of the world. Love goes all the way; love goes out of its way; love is the only way. To live a life of love which is the Way cuts across every bit of selfishness, as expressed in egotism, self-pity, self-enhancement and self-indulgence.

If we find ourselves, like Thomas, not sure what is the Way, then perhaps meditating on this poem by George Herbert may help.

> Come, my Way, my Truth, my Life:
> Such a Way, as gives us breath:
> Such a Truth, as ends all strife:
> Such a Life, as killeth death.

> Come, my Light, my Feast, my Strength:
> Such a Light, as shows a feast:
> Such a Feast, as mends in length:
> Such a Strength, as makes his guest.

> Come, my Joy, my Love, my Heart:
> Such a Joy, as none can move:

Such a Love, as none can part:
Such a Heart, as joys in love.[47]

Dear Lord, may I truly know that You are the only way that gives eternal life and leads to our true native land. Let me forsake anything which prevents me from following You as the Way, the Truth and Life. Amen.

[44] Andrewes, op. cit., Vol. 2, p.195.
[45] Ibid., Vol. 3, p.75.
[46] Julian of Norwich, *Revelations of Divine Love* (London, 1877), p.205.
[47] G. Herbert, op. cit., Vol. 2, p.178.

Saturday after the Fourth Sunday of Easter

Victory

The Lord has made His victory known;
He has displayed His saving righteousness to all the nations.

Psalm 98:2

Full readings: Acts 13:44-52; Psalm 98:1-4; St. John 14:7-14.

Christ's victory over death and darkness never rings so loud and lovingly as it does at the Easter Vigil with the chanting of the *Exsultet*. In this the deacon proclaims, on this most wonderful night, every victory Christ has won for us:

> He has ransomed us with His blood,
> and paid for us the price of Adam's sin
> to our eternal Father.

> This is our passover feast,
> when Christ, the true Lamb, is slain,
> whose blood consecrates the home of all believers.

> This is the night when Jesus Christ
> broke the chains of death
> and rose triumphant from the grave.

On this 'night truly blessed when heaven is wedded to earth and man is reconciled with God', the deacon is also proclaiming that all these victories gained by Christ are for all mankind. Salvation is assured to all who desire it through Christ. In today's lesson, as Paul and Barnabas continue their preaching in Antioch in Pisidia, it was made all too clear that those who desired eternal life would find it. Thus, in contrast to the Jews of that region who rejected Christ, the Gentiles were 'overjoyed' to hear of the 'means of salvation', and 'thankfully acclaimed the word of the Lord'. Through them the proclamation of the Easter Vigil was heard further afield.

We rejoice with all the choirs of angels on Easter Night that 'Jesus Christ, our King, is risen', and therefore we can 'sound the trumpet of salvation'. We thank God for His victory over all darkness within this world, and the knowledge that we too can share in His victory. We find ourselves getting so caught up with the overall picture of being redeemed from sin and the promise of new life in the Risen Lord, that we sometimes overlook the way by which we share in Christ's victory. We can only really share in this by conquering our individual sins, one by one. All of us have besetting sins, and if we have made our Paschal confession then we are quite aware of what these are. The new life of the Resurrection means taking these, and in the power of the Risen Lord to set out to be victorious over them. For example, our neglect of our nightly prayers; our irritability first thing in the morning; our over-indulgence of food or watching television; or our lack of concern and help for our next-door neighbour. We all should be aware of our sins of commission and omission. Sometimes it is easy to feel penitent for our sins in a general way, but real penitence always involves sorrow for our individual sins and amendment of life. Christ's victory over sin cost Him dearly; and so our victories over our besetting sins will also be costly, some more than others. But what is that cost in real terms when we compare it with spending eternity with the Glorified Lord? Isn't it worth it to sacrifice what we call a little pleasure here, for the pleasure we receive in conquering sin for Christ and to have the pleasure of living with Him forever? All so-called worldly pleasures are hollow and fleeting anyway. If we seek the virtues of the Kingdom of Heaven, such as love, humility, patience and long-suffering, all shown to us by Christ in His victory, then each moment of our lives will manifest Christ's victory to all. Above all, we shall truly share in the Paschal victory, and taste of its true joy. A Celtic poet, in his poem *Christ the King*, expresses this victory very simply in the following verse:

Because His hands knew torment,
Because He rose from the grave,
Let us ask our God on high,
There, where He bought us heaven,
Ask the Father, dear Saviour,
Jesus is called full of grace,
Watch over us, bring all men,
Our refuge, home to heaven.[48]

Through Your Spirit, O Risen Saviour, I can conquer all my besetting sins. Give me an ardent determination to be victorious over them
by amending my life to Your scrutiny, so that I can truly share in Your
glorious victory. Amen.

[48] Clancy, *Medieval Lyrics*, p.132.

The Fifth Sunday of Easter

A Royal Priesthood

But you are a chosen race, a royal priesthood, a dedicated nation, a people claimed by God for His own, to proclaim the glorious deeds of Him who has called you out of darkness into His marvellous light.

1 Peter 2:9

Full readings: Acts 6:1-7; Psalm 33; 1 Peter 2:4-9; St. John 14:1-12.

When we affirmed our Baptismal vows at the great Easter Vigil we may have been aware that this initiation rite into the Church sets us on a new course. We no longer belong to this world, in the sense of its worldliness, but have been made members of Christ's Kingdom. Consequently this initiation makes us members of another race, what St. Peter calls, in today's second reading, 'a chosen race'. The sign given to us to show we belong to this 'chosen race' was the cross made on our foreheads at our Baptism. This cross can never be erased. Once we have been made Christians we can never revert to being pagans. Perhaps we may become lapsed or lazy Christians, but never pagans again. Gregory of Narek, writing in the tenth century, captures this truth:

> With the seal of the cross,
> impressed with Your blood,
> with which we have been baptized
> to make us ready for adoption,
> You have modelled us into the image of Your glory.[49]

As a member of the royal priesthood, Peter emphasizes that God claims us for His very own. This means we are able to share in the eternal priesthood of Christ who, after His Ascension, is our High Priest in Heaven where He constantly intercedes on our behalf to the Father. We are also part of this royal priesthood because Christ, in having offered up Himself to the Father, now bestows the gift of grace upon all who belong to Him through Baptism. Thus it is through Baptism we are able to participate in His priesthood and all the benefits obtained from that. Although Baptism gives us our entry to share in the eternal priesthood of the Risen Saviour, it is in the other main sacrament, the Eucharist, that we are especially blessed through Christ's priestly life. In His office as the heavenly Priest, He perpetually pleads for us here on earth as we offer the eucharistic oblation day by day. Here we receive daily 'the Bread of Life', once broken for us on Calvary.

Have we ever thought very much about the priesthood being given to us? If we have not, this Easter is a good time to start meditating on what is expected of us as members of 'the royal priesthood'. Origen gives us a pretty good idea of what is involved. We 'ought to offer to God a sacrifice of praise, of prayers, of pity, of purity, of righteousness, [and] of holiness.' He also adds we 'must have the divine fire, God's own fire which He gives to men, of which the Son of God says, *I have come to send fire on earth.*'[50] It also means fulfilling our role as intercessor. Just as Christ intercedes for His Church so we too must intercede on behalf of our brethren at each Eucharist. We represent all those who do not or who are unable to join in the holy Sacrifice in their parish church. It is important to remember that we do not offer the Mass simply to save our own souls.

Our priestly role in this world also reminds us that we belong to a community which, in Christian terms, is the body of Christ, in which we share the gifts we have been given. It is essential for us to realise that each of us has a gift which has been especially given, but, and this is the important aspect, not simply for self indulgence, but to be used, shared and enjoyed by the whole community. Nothing is exclusively mine. This of course emphasizes our interdependence on each other at the expense of our independence. We have to accept there is no such thing as individuality within the royal priesthood, nor is there any thought of redundancy. Every cog in the wheel is essential. Therefore everyone has a special gift which is his or her giving. For example, the women who wash and press the altar linen are offering their work in unison with the priest as he celebrates the Holy Mysteries.

St. Peter also informs us of a further duty as members of this 'chosen race'–we must 'proclaim the glorious deeds of Him who has called you out of darkness into His marvellous light.' That is, we should follow the example of the Apostolic Church which, after the feast of Pentecost, never ceased from proclaiming the glorious deeds God has done, and their sharing of the life of the Risen Lord within them. What they were experiencing they wanted others to have too. As we draw closer to the Ascension and make our preparation for it, part of our preparation should be to ask ourselves do our hearts so burn for Christ that we want others to feel this in their lives? Is the Spirit of the Risen Lord a powerful force within us? Is it strong enough to challenge us and to arouse us out of any complacency? Am I indeed proclaiming the glorious Gospel, and thanking God for all His blessings in my witnessing? Furthermore, am I a responsible member of the royal priesthood? If we are not sure how to answer these questions, we need to re-evaluate our understanding of the role of the priesthood in relation to Christ and ourselves. We must firmly believe that we are members of the 'royal priesthood' by virtue of our Baptism.

Through my Baptism I was made a member of Your 'chosen race', and given a share in the eternal priesthood of the Risen Lord; let me show my gratitude in proclaiming Your love and goodness wherever I am. Amen.

[49] Berselli, op. cit., p.134.
[50] Bettensen, *Early Fathers*, p.251.

Monday after the Fifth Sunday of Easter

The Teacher

'The Holy Spirit whom the Father will send in my name,
will teach you everything and remind you of all that I
have told you.'

St. John 14:26

Full readings: Acts 14:5-18; Psalm 114:1-4, 15-16; St. John 14:21-6.

Before and after His Crucifixion and Resurrection, Jesus made it
abundantly clear to His disciples that, if He were to be with them
always, He must ascend to His Father in order to send the Holy Spirit
who would abide with them forever as Teacher, Comforter and Guide.
Although before the first Pentecost the apostles were rather sceptical of
this, after that day of Pentecost they never doubted for one moment the
meaning of Our Lord's teaching on the outpouring of the Holy Spirit.
The Spirit of Christ was all too manifest in their lives. They who had
been timid, afraid and reticent were now filled with a boldness and
resolution previously unexperienced. Today's lesson, telling us of Paul
and Barnabas' ministry in Lycaonia, is indicative of this. Such were the
manifestations of the Spirit through this ministry that the local people
were convinced they must have been gods rather than doing the work
of the one Almighty God.

The Holy Spirit taught members of the early Church the essence of
Christ's teaching, and so time and time again we hear them reiterating
what Jesus had told them on Easter Day, that His death and Resurrection were but a fulfilment of God's plan for His people as outlined by

the prophets. As Hildegard of Bingen explains it:

> And the Holy Spirit took their human fear from them,
> so that no dread was in them, and they would never fear
> human savagery when they spoke the word of God; all
> such timidity was taken from them, so ardently and so
> quickly that they became firm and not soft, and dead
> to all adversity that could befall them. And then they
> remembered with perfect understanding all the things
> they had heard and received from Christ with sluggish
> faith and comprehension; they recalled them to memory
> as if they had learned them from Him in that very
> hour.[51]

Our Lord taught over and over again that He was many essential things in His great '*I am*'s.' I am the Truth and the Bread of Life, for example. However, it is only through the working of the Holy Spirit that we can ever acknowledge that Jesus is indeed the Truth and the Bread of Life. Jesus, in this chapter from St. John's Gospel from which today's Gospel reading comes, also commands us to love Him and to love His commandments. This, we know from our own experiences, is no easy task. However, by not being easy we realize it is something we can never do through our own efforts. It can only be achieved by something more lovely and holier than us. Hence we acknowledge we can only love through the active existence of the Spirit within us.

A couple of days ago the Gospel reading from St. John emphasized that it is only when we are reborn in the Spirit that we can have the life abundant that Jesus speaks of so much in His ministry. To live abundantly and richly in Christ is all that any Christian can ever desire, but to be able to seek and experience that, it is a gift of the Holy Spirit. As we approach the feast of Pentecost let us pray constantly that the Holy Spirit will grant to us this gift too, and that He will be our Teacher and Guide throughout each day.

For so long the Holy Spirit has been neglected in traditional Christianity, and perhaps even today we tend to think of it only in *charismatic* terms. This, however, is to make nonsense of all Christ's teaching. How often did He teach that He and the Spirit with the Father are all one; They are active in creation, redemption and sanctification every moment. The Spirit is continually hovering over creation; He is continually teaching us the truth; He is continually filling our being with love; He is continually instructing us in the virtues of the kingdom. Indeed, the Holy Spirit can teach quietly, but He can also make His presence rather noticeable and noisy. Sometimes we need the latter; we need to be disturbed and perturbed by His noisome presence in order to break out of our lethargy.

Jesus makes it clear that unless we allow the Spirit to be our teacher, we shall never come to know the Father. If we deny the Holy Spirit giving us this knowledge we shall never be able to come to Our Father and make our everlasting 'dwelling with Him'. We must listen to what are the Father's words for us through the operation of the Holy Spirit through Christ.

O Holy Spirit, who testifies to the teaching of Our Lord Jesus Christ, fill me with Your gifts, so that I can be Your vehicle as Your teacher, comforter and guide in this world. Amen.

---

[51] Hildegard of Bingen, *Scivias*, trans. Mother Columba Hart and Janet Bishop (The Classics of Western Spirituality, New York, 1990), p.415.

Tuesday after the Fifth Sunday of Easter

Parting Gift

'Peace is my parting gift to you, my own peace, such as
the world cannot give. Set your troubled hearts at rest,
and banish your fears.'

St. John 14:27

Full readings: Acts 14:19-28; Psalm 145:10-13, 21; St. John 14:27-31.

Christ's parting gift to His disciples before all the agony of His
Passion was peace. Peace is something we all pursue. We all desire so
desperately to be at peace with ourselves. Perhaps we don't care too
much about being at peace with others or what man does to his fellow
man by varying degrees of acts in violence every day in so many places
of this globe, but we do care about our inner peace. Indeed, we so want
our minds free of scorpions that, if we cannot be free of such torment,
some of us opt out of life altogether, either through drugs, alcohol, or
even suicide.

Yet peace is a bit like happiness; it can never be bought like buying
chocolate from a slot machine. They both come from the way we live; it
is more a question of *how* we live rather than *why* we live. If our lives
are Christ-centred then we shall experience in varying degrees the kind
of peace Our Lord promises here.

What kind of peace did Jesus promise His disciples? It certainly was
not the kind of peace this world suggests, where peace is often taken as
meaning a feeling of security and comfort. No, Christ's peace is far
more complex than this. If we recall when this discourse took place, we

shall realize it was before all hell broke loose for Christ. So between this guarantee of peace by Christ, and His bestowing His peace upon them after His Resurrection, is the Cross. On the Cross Our Lord bore all the violence, hatred, malice and spitefulness, not only inflicted upon Him at Gethesemane, Gabbatha and Golgotha, but He absorbed into His Body every act of violence man commits against his fellow man. Thus Christ turns the Cross into a peace-making witness as He accomplishes the will of His Father. Thus the peace which Christ gives is the assurance that above all suffering, pain and destruction there is something stronger and lasting. Rowan Williams expresses Christ's gift of peace like this:

> For him, passing through the cross is the final peace-making. It establishes in the world of men and women the truth of an affirmation and acceptance beyond all our destructiveness, untruth and pain, telling us that we may have a Father also–that we may be trustingly surrendered to the source of our life and life of all things, and receive into our minds and hearts the stillness of Jesus' offering of himself, the peace of the cross. It will not take away inner or outer conflict; on the contrary it will force us into conflict, into battle for the sake of truth we have been given.[52]

Experiencing 'the peace of the Cross' in our lives enables us to cope with things even in its most chaotic, frenzied, darkened and dreadful moments, because there is always a way through. How often did Mother Julian of Norwich say, 'All is well, and all will be well.' Many times, because through the Cross and the empty tomb all is well. However, don't expect those who live only to this world or see everything against them to understand this. Only a Christian who has truly committed his or her life to Christ knows what joy comes from 'the peace of God which passes all understanding'. That is why the persecutors of the early Christians could not understand how the disciples joyfully underwent all kinds of persecution as we read in today's lesson, or how the saints like Polycarp, Ignatius and Perpetua and Felicity ran to receive the crown of martyrdom. Polycarp's last prayer is an example of a soul at peace:

I praise You for everything, I bless You, I glorify You, through the eternal and heavenly High Priest Jesus Christ Your beloved Son, through whom be glory to You together with Him and the Holy Spirit, both now and for the ages yet to come.[53]

If at the moment we find our lives in such turmoil that it seems to control us, ponder on the meaning of 'the peace of the Cross', Our Lord's parting gift to us. Let the Cross absorb everything which disturbs and troubles us. Although our lives may not be any less 'peaceful', we shall nevertheless experience the *pax* of Christ, triumphant over all the worst that this world can inflict in our inner life.

When we reflect on Our Lord's parting gift of peace, we are very much aware of the need for peace amongst all those who live in fear of their lives in so many troubled spots of this world. There are just so many places where people simply hate one another without knowing why. So we as Christians must pray daily for peace to dwell in the heart of every person on this earth, so that all thoughts of violence, retribution and hate may be driven from them by the Spirit of Love. 'My peace I give unto you' must touch the hearts of everyone. Can we make it an act of discipline? If not already so, let us pray daily for peace to dwell in the hearts of all men, and to learn to love rather than hate in every situation.

Thank you, my Risen Saviour, for Your parting gift of peace, a peace You give me through Calvary. May Your peace enable me to meet all the trials, storms and tribulations of this life cheerfully, and let me be an instrument of Your peace in this world. Amen.

[52] R.D. Williams, *The Truce of God* (London, 1983), pp.82-3.
[53] St. Polycarp, *The Epistles and The Martyrdom of St. Polycarp* (The Works of The Fathers, London, 1948), Vol. 6, p.97.

Wednesday after the Fifth Sunday of Easter

The True Vine

'I am the true vine, and my Father is the gardener....
I am the vine; you are the branches. Anyone who dwells
in me, as I dwell in him, bears much fruit; apart from me
you can do nothing.'

St. John 15:1, 5

Full readings: Acts 15:1-6; Psalm 122:1-5; St. John 15:1-8.

In yet another one of the well known *I ams*, Christ manifests the
unity between Himself and the Father, and teaches that the same unity
between Himself and His Father should exist between him and us. In
all His farewell discourses Jesus emphasized how He and His Father are
one: 'Believe me when I say that I am in the Father and the Father in
me'; the Father will send the Holy Spirit 'in my name'; 'I go unto My
Father'; and so on. If we are a little dismayed about trying to understand the relationship among the three Persons of the Godhead,
remember so were the disciples. They too found it puzzling when their
Master taught about the relationship between Himself and His Father.

When Jesus told them He was returning to His Father's house, we
hear Philip pleading to be shown the Father. Jesus replies almost
despairingly, 'Have I been all this time with you, Philip, and still you do
not know me? Anyone who has seen me has seen the Father.' (Jn.
14:9). And then on his discourse of the vine and branches, He informs
them that the Father is the gardener, discarding any barren branch,
while He is the vine.

95

In this discourse Our Lord makes it abundantly clear that He is the Vine, we are the branches but the Father is the source of all life; the branches can only bear fruit if they are united to the vine. However, the quantity and quality of the fruit depend very much on the pruning of the branches by the gardener who is His Father. Both the Son and Father are united in giving life and fruitfulness. However, any branch which withers because it severs itself from the Vine, is 'gathered up, thrown on the fire, and burnt' by the gardener.

To live that abundant life which Christ offers, it must be lived through Him in unity with the Father because 'They are one, and work inseparably with each other.' This unity between Father and Son also extends to the Holy Spirit. 'The Father does not work without the Son, nor the Son without the Holy Spirit, nor the Holy Spirit without Them, nor the Father and the Son without the Holy Spirit, but They are undivided unity.'[54]

'By their fruits you shall know them,' Jesus also told His disciples. Today's Gospel challenges us to look at what quality and quantity of fruit our life is bearing at present. Is the harvest very meagre or is it abundant; is the fruit bitter or sweet; is the fruit ripe or green; do the branches need pruning or are they in fact starting to wither? Answering these questions is a bit like a daily self-examination routine, but one which must be done if we honestly desire to live a more Christ-like existence. Nothing is plainer than Christ's warning that there can be no life, that is, real living without Him. His discourse here links assuredly with His discourse on the Bread of Life. 'I am the living Bread.' That Bread, the staff of our life, is offered and given to us day by day. It is the receiving of that Life which makes our branches not barren but fruitful; it changes everything into being lively. Ephrem the Syrian illustrates this 'extraordinary greatness' in his Maundy Thursday hymnody:

> Blessed are you, O holy place, where our Lord broke the bread that had become His body. The narrow refuge opened out to the whole world, which was entirely conquered by it; with Moses there came from the glorious mountain top a covenant to last but a short time; from this modest abode, instead, there came a pact of extraordinary greatness that changed the whole world.[55]

Undoubtedly the life of Christ flowing from the Father, through the Spirit, once it enters us, will automatically change our lives, and make them too places 'of extraordinary greatness'.

O blessed Trinity, the Giver of all life, help me never to sever my branch from the Vine, so that Your life will always flow, enabling a plentiful harvest of sweet fruit. Amen.

[54] Hildegard, op. cit., p.419.
[55] Berselli, op. cit., p.66.

Thursday after the Fifth Sunday of Easter

The First Council

'In my judgement, therefore, we should impose no irksome restrictions on those of the Gentiles who are turning to God.'

Acts 15:19

Full readings: Acts 15:7-21; Psalm 96:1-3, 10; St. John 15:9-11.

We have seen during our series of meditations how many of the Christian Jews objected to the Gospel being preached to the Gentiles. Even Peter had questioned this until God taught him that the Good News must be preached to all. Now after many Gentiles had become Christian, especially through the missionary work of Barnabas and Paul, some Jewish believers of the Pharisaic party were insisting that Gentiles who were baptized should also be circumcised and thus keep the law of Moses. If only they had realized how negative was this thinking. Hadn't Christ absorbed the Old Covenant into the New? They still had not realized that 'for anyone united to Christ, there is a new creation: the old order has gone; a new order has already begun.' (2 Cor. 5:17).

So contentious was this issue that the Church in Antioch decided to send Barnabas, Paul and others to Jerusalem to debate this with Peter, James and other leading Christians there.

This meeting of the leading Christians in Jerusalem led to what we recognize as the first council of the Church. Leading the debate was Peter who insisted that it was God's will that the Holy Spirit was given to the Gentiles just as it was given to the Jews. Indeed 'He made no difference between them and us.' (Acts 15:8-9) If that is so, why enforce 'a yoke' on them which is not necessary for salvation? After all, we are all 'saved in the same way,...by the grace of the Lord Jesus' (Acts 15:11).

Supporting Peter were Barnabas and Paul who, in outlining their ministry to the Gentiles, 'described all the signs and portents that God had worked' amongst them. After listening to the reports, James, as chairman, gave his judgment. This judgment wisely freed the Gentiles of any 'irksome restrictions', and made it clear that in Christ alone was salvation, and that the only initiation rite needed for the Gentile was Baptism. In Baptism the Gentile as well as the Jew was made a member of Christ and an inheritor of the kingdom of God. All Christians were made brothers in Christ. Thus the decision of this council in Jerusalem guaranteed that the Gentiles would continue to receive the Gospel without any *strings attached.*

This issue discussed at Jerusalem is still relevant today. It is really very easy to be a Pharisaic Christian because time and time again we find ourselves being tied down to conventional ways, or the way something is to be done because that is the way it has always been done. However, the Holy Spirit does not work like that. He breaks through or He wants to break through all the 'yokes' we place in His way. The Holy Spirit is the breath of fresh air which wants to stir us out of our staleness; or the morning dew which refreshes our parchedness; or the bright sun which penetrates our gloominess. We have to learn it is the Spirit who directs!

Then there is the Pharisaic approach to our prayer life. We can rigidly adhere to saying prayers, perhaps a certain number each day, without ever giving a thought about to whom we are offering them. The same is possible with our worship on Sunday. We can blithely say the Liturgy with our thoughts a thousand miles away, and not be caught up with the Eucharistic actions at all. We can go through all the motions without really giving time to, and being with the Lord. There are so many different ways we can wear the Pharisaic yoke around our neck, and thus stifle any working of the Holy Spirit. We must never forget the Risen Lord makes us free and fresh, and in the spirit of Christ there is a spontaneity of living.

The first council at Jerusalem also warns us against restricting the working of the Holy Spirit through what we recognize as the proper channels. We must never forget that the Spirit is always hovering and brooding over His world. We cannot tell from whence the Spirit comes or where it goes. 'Whoever is not against me is with me,' said Jesus. We have to be prepared to recognize manifestations of the Spirit, many of which will be outside our own experiences. We can never put limits or labels on the Spirit as He wanders where He will. Indeed, as Michael Ramsey reminds us, 'the Church [only] exists by the power of the Holy Spirit. Whether as fellowship, or body, or temple, or people of God, it has no existence apart from the impact of the Holy Spirit upon human lives.'[56] So we must try to live so that we never do anything to stifle or hinder the free-flowing Spirit, but allow Him to take us wherever He beckons.

O Holy Spirit, free me from any kind of Pharisaic approach to my living out the Christian life. Let my life be as spontaneous as You want it to be. Amen.

[56] M. Ramsey, *Holy Spirit* (London, 1977), p.84.

Friday after the Fifth Sunday of Easter

Encouragement

When it was read, all rejoiced at the encouragement it brought, and Judas and Silas, who were themselves prophets, said much to encourage and strengthen the members.

Acts 15:31-2

Full readings: Acts 15:22-31; Psalm 57:8-12; St. John 15:12-17.

I have often stated that, as Christians, we are members of Christ's Church and therefore we belong to a community in which we share what we are and what we have with the other members. Part of that sharing results in strengthening one another. Yet true strengthening can only happen if our sharing also includes encouragement. Encouragement means exuding warmth and making others feel they are strengthened. However, encouragement to our fellow sisters and brothers is unfortunately overlooked at times. We are sometimes reasonably good about sharing our goods and talents, but recognizing the need for encouragement and support can only come when we truly are aware of another person and his/her predicament. In any community there will always be those who are not as strong as others, or feel they have to be freed from their feelings of despair and utter helplessness, or who need an extra hand as it were; or who simply need reassuring in their faith, daily work or even that they are on the right track as it were in what they are doing. Part of our work as Christians is to cheer and comfort others.

In today's lesson we see the outcome of encouragement as we read of how the Christian communities in Antioch, Syria and Celicia were able to grow, not only numerically but in strength because of the Council of Jerusalem's decision to send them a message, freeing them from any kind of censure in not observing the laws of Moses at the hands of two holy disciples, Judas and Silas. Through the ministry of these two and the recommendations set out by the Council, the Christians in these places were greatly encouraged to continue preaching the Gospel of Christ. The original work of Paul and Barnabas was consolidated, and the Church in Antioch grew from strength to strength. The Christians in Antioch had learnt how to encourage one another in living unto Christ.

Can we follow their example? In today's Gospel reading we are exhorted by Christ to carry out 'My commandment'. That commandment is 'to love one another, as I have loved you' (Jn. 15:12). Unfortunately, for many 'love of [our] brother consists, not in helping [our] brother to grow and mature in love as an individual person loved by Christ, but in making him *toe the line* and fulfil exterior obligations, without any regard for the interior need of his soul for love, understanding and communion.'[57] Of course, such an approach towards another person is the enemy of Christ, the enemy of Love, and obviously destroys any kind of workable relationship. As Merton explained:

> This is in reality a fatal perversion of the Christian spirit. Such 'love' is the enemy of the Cross of Christ because it flatly contradicts the teaching and the mercy of Christ. It treats man as if he were made for the sabbath.[58]

To love one another involves not only giving but being sensitive to others and their needs. This means we should be aware of the need of giving a word of encouragement when it is needed. Indeed, the very way we live should in itself be an encouragement to all we meet. It will be if we have completely surrendered ourselves to the working of the Holy Spirit through us. When we do that we discover that Love overflows. The Indian spiritual thinker, Swami Ramdas, reminds us that 'love begets love'. There are no exceptions to this law. 'When our love goes to [people] and their love comes to us, the two streams mingle together and there is an ocean of love and joy. . . . It is a spontaneous merging of souls.'[59] We have all experienced this is what happens indeed, when our actions have brought encouragement to another. There remains a bond forever. When we reflect back on our own lives we discover many bonds have been made because people took the trouble to encourage us in whatever we were doing. I have always thought that the prime duty of a teacher and parent is to encourage and inspire, even if there seems very little basis on which to do this at the time. It is all too easy to denounce and criticize negatively or to impose the unattainable, but that is not Christ's way. He meets people where they are, and unveils that potential. If the Council of Jerusalem had imposed the rigid laws of Moses upon the Gentiles, it probably would have divided the early Church quite damagingly. The important factor we take from today's readings is that encouragement, not condemnation, is the way of Christ in our community living.

O Holy Spirit, so inspire me with Your gifts that my life will continually be one of encouragement to all I meet. Through it may others be brought to know and love You. Amen.

[57] T. Merton, *The Power and Meaning of Love* (London, 1976), p.20.
[58] Ibid.
[59] S. Ramdas, from *Thus Speaks Ramdas*, in *Prayers for Peace*, eds. R. Runcie and B. Hume (London, 1987), p.38.

Saturday after the Fifth Sunday of Easter

The Second Missionary Journey

As they made their way from town to town they handed on the decisions taken by the apostles and elders in Jerusalem and enjoined their observance. So, day by day, the churches grew stronger in faith and increased in numbers.

Acts 16:4-5

Full readings: Acts 16:1-10; Psalm 100:1-3, 5; St. John 15:18-21.

Today's lesson tells of the beginning of what is known as the second missionary journey of Paul. The ministry which he had shared with Barnabas came to an abrupt end as they planned their return 'to see how our brothers are getting on in the various towns where we proclaimed the word of the Lord.' (Acts 15:36). Their sad parting was over John Mark who accompanied them on their first journey as far as Pamphylia from where he returned to Jerusalem. Barnabas wanted Mark to accompany them, but Paul was adamant that he would not. So 'sharp' was their quarrel that Paul and Barnabas separated; Paul took Silas, one of the prophets from Jerusalem with him, while Barnabas with Mark sailed to Cyprus.

As St. Paul began this second missionary journey, there are significant factors. The first is at Lystra. Here he discovers Timothy, a Christian whose mother is a Christian Jew and father a Gentile. One of the crucial points of discussion at the Council of Jerusalem had been whether Gentile Christians had to undergo the Jewish rite of circumcision. Wisely the Council rejected this, but here we find Paul having Timothy circumcised 'out of consideration for the Jews who lived in those parts' (Acts 16:3). Is Paul implying here that the law of charity always overrides everything else? I think he is, otherwise the circumcision in the circumstance does not make sense. If Timothy's circumcision is an example of charity being the highest virtue of all, then it challenges all our rigidities. Sometimes it is a very hard lesson for us to learn that most rules can be broken in the name of charity. This was brought home to me on a Friday during Lent this year when I was invited as the special guest by my Bangladeshi student to celebrate the ending of Ramadan. For me, as it is indeed for many Christians, Friday, especially in Lent, is a day of fasting and self-denial. However, I realized it was a great honour for my student and her family to entertain me, so I had to accept graciously that their hospitality meant eating enormously from the ten or more special dishes they had prepared. As I tried to plough through all this food, I thought, Saturday can be my Friday this week! After all, their joy in being able to give was the most *Christian* factor at that moment. Moreover, Our Lord had warned us we must never become enslaved to laws just for the sake of observing them.

The other significant factor is that Paul and Silas constantly travelled to where the Spirit led them. The Spirit prevented them from entering Asia, because He wanted them to go to Macedonia. At that particular moment it was crucial for Silas and Paul to be in Greece. Whether we realize it or not, the Spirit is doing the same thing in our lives. Perhaps most times this goes unnoticed, but every now and again something happens when we see all too clearly the result of being led. Each one of us can look back and see, often vividly, where the Spirit has led us in order to do His work.

The more we grow in living with Christ, where His and our lives seem to merge, where prayer and work seem to fuse, the more we understand this being led by the Spirit. Being confident in that means there is no preoccupation with the ideas of security for the future because we believe that God does provide, provided we earnestly seek His will. Being led by the Spirit means we are too living out the work of a missionary. So many of us have always believed that a missionary is someone who takes the Good News to another continent. However, a missionary is one who is sent, sent by the Holy Spirit to wherever He directs. This usually is not in some obscure corner of the globe but here locally within our own community. It is here that the Gospel needs to be preached too. We sometimes forget this!

The Gospel for today underlines this sense of direction when Jesus warned His disciples and us that the worldly will find such thinking foolish and they may even hate and persecute us because of it. However, we do not have to concern ourselves about this, as the world has already expressed its hatred to Our Lord, and anything we suffer is for Him. As St. Paul says, we are glad to be fools for Christ's sake, to suffer and to endure. He certainly wrote from his own experiences as we discover during this second missionary journey, and before his life was spent he endured many more sufferings and afflictions.

The other important fact which we learn from this journey is that we must constantly pray to do God's will. St. Francis of Assisi, in his reflection on *The Lord's Prayer*, commends this prayer on the petition *Thy will be done*:

> May [we] love You with our whole heart by always thinking of You; with our whole soul by always desiring You; with all our mind by always directing our intention to You, and seeking Your glory in all things, and with all our strength by employing all the powers and senses of our soul and body in the service of Your love, and in nothing else; and that we may love our neighbour as ourselves, drawing all to Your love with all our power, rejoicing in the good of others as in our own, compassionating them in their troubles, and giving offence to no-one.[60]

O blessed Spirit, so possess and direct me that I may be Your instrument wherever You send me. Teach me not to reject or despise any situations where You have sent me, but to allow Love to embrace everything. Amen.

---

[60] St. Francis of Assisi, op. cit., p.170.

The Sixth Sunday of Easter

The Spirit of Truth

'I will ask the Father, and He will give you another to be
your advocate, who will be with you forever–the Spirit of
truth.'

St. John 14:16-17

Full readings: Acts 8:5-8, 14-17; Psalm 66; 1 Peter 3:15-18; St. John
14:15-21.

Today's Gospel proclaims the wonderful news of Jesus' assurance
that He will never leave us. He, through the presence of the Holy
Spirit, will live within us forever. Furthermore, through the Spirit we
will be given the gift of truth 'which will teach [us] all things', and which
will be a source of great comfort because 'you will know that I live in
you and you in me'. You will indeed know that 'I am the Truth'. As
Frank explained:

> His word is truth, and guides us into that, into the true
> understanding and practice of it. . . . He shows us the
> Father, he reveals to us the Son; he interprets the words
> and writes it in our hearts; he leads and upholds us by his
> promises, seals them unto us, seals us again to the day of
> redemption, the day of truth, the day when all things will
> appear truly as they are.[61]

As this discourse on His promise to be always with His disciples was given before His Crucifixion, it manifests Jesus' utmost empathy with them. What will they feel when He is condemned to die? He earnestly desired His followers to realize that what was before Him would not mean the end of His being with them. His presence would not cease even with His death at Calvary, 'I shall not leave you bereft; I am coming back to you.' (Jn. 14:18). After His Resurrection He continues the same theme. Mary Magdalen's message to the disciples was that not only has Christ risen, but He is also ascending to His Father. He is going away again, but not parting from them. He must physically leave them in order to be with them forever. He has promised to send them the Comforter, and today we have seen He will also send 'the Spirit of truth'. The Father will do this in His name. Once again we see the unity of the Trinity in the giving of gifts of the Spirit.

With Ascension Day this coming Thursday, our thoughts during the next few days should very much concentrate on what this means in relation to Christ's own teaching. He taught the apostles that, although they would grieve with His leaving them by returning to His heavenly home, He must if He is going to abide with them forever. He had to go home to His Father in order that the Holy Spirit could be sent to them. This in reality would be His living presence dwelling within them. Thus they could be assured that the living Christ would always abide in them and be the guiding force in their ministry.

He further assures the disciples that 'you will see me', even when He returns to His Father. By this He meant through their faith they would always behold Him; He would be as real to them in His spiritual presence as He was in His physical abode with them during the last three years. And of course He was and is; the Apostolic Church is a testimony to the disciples' living with Jesus. He was as real to them as He always had been, probably more real as their lives burned and glowed with the Truth. Jesus as the Spirit of Truth spoke through them as they preached the Good News of Salvation to all.

Today's reading from Acts tells us how that Spirit of Truth was given through Peter and John to those Samaritans who believed in Christ, after the preaching of Philip and who were 'baptized into the name of the Lord Jesus'. However, the gifts of the Spirit were not given simultaneously. This they received through the laying on of hands by Peter and John. Just as these Samaritan Christians were filled with the Spirit of Truth, so are we at our baptism and confirmation along with the other gifts of the Spirit.

The Spirit of Truth is Christ Himself. That is why He promises to be with us forever. Having the Truth abiding in us will enable us to recognize and seek out the truth. Possession of Truth leads to abundancy of life because it rejects all hypocrisy, deceit and errors. That is what Christ meant when He said 'because I live, you too will live.' It is by possessing Truth that we shall be able not only to receive Christ's commands, but to obey them. When we obey His commands we are also loving Our Lord. That love will not go unrecognized because Jesus assures us that they who love God, both the Father and the Son, will love in a very special way.

What more wonderful news could we ever want to hear? This is the Ascension message: 'I am coming back to you.' We are no longer left to our own devices and muddle. There is a direction to everything. Not only do we possess the Truth to give this direction, but the Truth Himself has guaranteed that the Father will welcome us home as He welcomed His Son. We know that our presence is very much wanted there, and that is our glorious reward provided we stay faithful and obey Christ's commands.

Come and possess me, O blessed Spirit. Fill me with Truth so that I shall always want to obey Christ's commands. Thank you, O Lord, for not leaving me comfortless by giving me Your gifts through the Spirit, and for the assurance of Your everlasting presence. Amen.

[61] Frank, op. cit., Vol. 2, p.230.

Monday after the Sixth Sunday of Easter

Lydia

One of those listening was called Lydia, a dealer in purple fabric;...she was a worshipper of God and the Lord opened her heart to respond to what Paul said.

Acts 16:14

Full readings: Acts 16:11-15; Psalm 149:1-6, 9; St. John 15:26-16:4.

In yesterday's Gospel Jesus assured us that the Spirit of Truth was always abiding within us. Our Lord in the Gospel for today implicates us to respond to His presence. Just as the Spirit bears witness to the Son, so we in turn through the Spirit must bear witness to the Son. To inspire us in such witness we do not have to look any further than today's lesson from Acts. On this second missionary journey Paul and Silas had reached the city of Philippi where they encountered, during their preaching and ministry, Lydia, a seller of purple dyes. She was one of a number of women who met for prayer on the river bank, just outside the town. As a person who already believed in God, she was receptive to Paul's preaching, and afterwards she and her household were baptized. Immediately she put into practice the meaning of belonging to the Church, the Christian community, when she announced, 'Now that you have accepted me as a believer in the Lord, come and stay at my house.' (Acts 16:15). Such was her enthusiasm, Luke adds, 'And she insisted on our going.' If only we could show the same warmth and welcome! This was witness indeed to Christ, the Lord she had accepted through the Spirit. I can imagine her singing her praises from today's psalm as she set off home to make preparations:

Praise the Lord
Praise God in His holy place,
praise Him in the mighty vault of heaven;
praise Him for His acts of power,
praise Him for His immeasurable greatness.

(Ps. 150:1-2)

Her home became a centre for Christians to meet and hear the Word from Paul and Silas. Undoubtedly many were added to the faithful who witnessed for Christ in Philippi through Lydia's warm hospitality.

Jesus, however, warned the disciples, as He does us, that witnessing to Him will often lead to persecution and punishment because they who inflict these do 'not know either the Father or Me' (Jn. 16:3). Only those with whom the Spirit abides can ever understand the Word. So it is not surprising that we discover that, while staying in Philippi at Lydia's house, Paul and Silas are dragged into the city square by slave owners when their slave girl is released from demonic possession through Paul's command in the name of Jesus to come out 'instantly'. Evil, as Jesus taught, can never tolerate the truth; it never wants light to penetrate to reveal the works of darkness. So the slave owners could not stand such a witness to Truth, and continued their walking in darkness by hauling off Paul and Silas to the city's authorities.

Witnessing to the Spirit of Truth will invariably bring us up against many forms of darkness in this world. Sometimes this witness is achieved through prayer and self-denial, especially when darkness exists far from our home. One example of this darkness is in Northern Ireland, where Irish kill Irish irrationally. For this situation our prayers for love, reconciliation and peace are desperately needed daily. We also need to offer up acts of sacrifice for Truth to prevail in this darkened area of our world, as well as in many others, and for love to fill the hearts of all so that man will see his brother in a new perspective. Desmond Tutu has written 'When you look at someone with eyes of love, you see a reality different from that of someone who looks at the same person without love, with hatred or even just with indifference.'[62]

We also do need to speak out against any injustices in this world. As Christians we can never be passive bystanders. We shall indeed know whether the Spirit dwells in us because, if He does we shall never be afraid to speak out against all evil acts committed to humans, animals and nature. The Spirit of Truth makes us bold and fearless as were the disciples in the Apostolic Church. Luke's account of this Apostolic Church is really the Spirit of Truth in action.

O Spirit of Truth, glow within me so that all dross may be consumed within me. Being freed, let my life be a perpetual witness to Christ by always seeking the Truth and fighting against all evil. Amen.

[62] D. Tutu, *Hope and Suffering* (London, 1984), p.150.

Tuesday after the Sixth Sunday of Easter

The Gaoler

The gaoler called for lights, rushed in, and threw himself
down before Paul and Silas, trembling with fear. He then
escorted them out and said, 'Sirs, what must I do to be
saved?'

Acts 16:29-30

Full readings: Acts 16:22-34; Psalm 138:1-3, 7-8; St. John 16:5-11.

Extraordinary things continue to happen through the release of the
Spirit in the Apostolic Church. Despite their fierce flogging and
imprisonment in Philippi, Paul and Silas continued in their loud singing
of praises to God, only too glad to suffer for Christ. Such is their faith in
God that another miracle happens. A tremendous earthquake throws
the prison doors wide open, and the gaoler, on awakening, assuming
that the prisoners would have fled, went to commit suicide. However,
Paul shouted to him that everything was really all right as no-one had
tried to escape. The gaoler, seeing that Paul and Silas and the rest of
the prisoners, who undoubtedly had been touched by the faith of the
two disciples, had not tried to escape as most would have, sensed there
was a greater presence in the ruined gaol. Knowing that Paul and Silas
had been imprisoned because of their work in a special name, he
demands to know, 'What must I do to be saved?' (Acts 16:30). They
informed him that it is only through 'the Lord Jesus', in whose name
they have performed all their preaching and healing, that this can
happen. After preaching to him of the Gospel, the gaoler and his

113

household were baptized, but not before ministering to the physical needs of Paul and Silas by bathing their wounds. Indeed, this was a night of great rejoicing, beginning with the joyful songs of praise by Paul and Silas, and ending in the meal these two shared with the gaoler and his household in thanksgiving for the faith God had blessed them with that night. We can almost hear the gaoler offering up his praises in words from today's set psalm:

> Let all the kings of the earth praise you, Lord,
> when they hear the words You have spoken;
> let them sing of the Lord's ways
> for great is the glory of the Lord.
>
> (Ps. 138:4-5)

The rejoicing of this particular night, as we continue our own celebrations of the great Paschal wonders and joys forces us to reflect on how much rejoicing there should be in our lives for those 'inestimable benefits' and blessings we receive so abundantly. If we but reflect for a moment, we should acknowledge our lives are so rich in Christ, and therefore in the words of today's psalm:

> I shall give praise to You, Lord, with my whole heart;
> in the presence of the gods I shall sing psalms to you.
> I shall bow down towards Your holy temple;
> for Your love and faithfulness I shall praise Your name
> for You have exalted Your promise above the heavens.
>
> (Ps. 138:1-2)

What happened to the gaoler symbolizes the meaning of today's Gospel reading, in which Jesus is still hammering away that after His departure the Spirit of Truth will come. When He comes, 'He will prove the world wrong about sin, justice and judgment.' (Jn. 16:8). Living in his pagan world the gaoler had no real concept what was meant by any of these. However, as soon as he was confronted by Christ and filled with the Spirit he was able to recognize what these were. For instance, justice came to mean for him making amends for the maltreatment of Paul and Silas.

The Spirit of Truth casts a new dimension over everything. We see sin clearly for what it is: hurting God, others and ourselves. We see it as separating us from Our Lord and from others; we see it as destroying any kind of relationships, whether with God or others. It hinders and stunts any growth whatsoever, and it prevents us from having any real joy in our lives. Through Truth we can also recognize various acts of injustice committed by us and others in all parts of the world; we acknowledge that any kind of force and retaliation is contrary to God's concept of justice; we realize that love only overcomes all injustices. Furthermore, we comprehend that everything we do is continually being judged by how it measures against Truth, as we are continually being judged on the way we live day by day by the values of the heavenly Kingdom. Once we accept Christ wholeheartedly into our lives, we are very much aware we are continually being judged by the One whose Manhood intercedes for us perpetually in heaven.

By allowing our lives to be continually searched out and pierced by the Spirit of Truth means we can never continue for very long behind any façade, sham, pretence, dishonesty or illusion. We are able to look reality into the face and accept who we are and what we are and what we can become in the living power of the Ascended Lord.

O blessed Trinity, fill my heart with never-ceasing praise for all your love, goodness and mercies to me day by day. Through the Spirit of Truth may all that is contrary to the Spirit of Love be revealed to me, and then acknowledged by me so that You may work and shine through all I do. Amen.

Wednesday after the Sixth Sunday of Easter

Worship

As I was going round looking at the objects of your worship, I noticed among other things an altar bearing the inscription 'To an unknown God'. What you worship but do not know—this is what I now proclaim.

Acts 17:23

Full readings: Acts 17:15, 22-18:1; Psalm 148:1-2, 11-14; St. John 16:12-15.

The Athenians were great worshippers, not of the true and only God, but of many gods. Consequently their city was full of idols, much to Paul's horror who spent his time in Athens arguing against the worship of these various deities. The Athenians were intrigued to hear about another new 'god', especially One who had risen from death. Thus Paul found himself speaking before the Council of Areopagus about 'this new doctrine'.

Paul's aim was to convince these Athenians they were mistaken in whom they worshipped. Instead they should be transferring their worship to the Lord Jesus who is the 'unknown God', honoured upon one of their altars. Paul, full of the Spirit of Truth himself, desires fervently that that same Spirit will penetrate the hearts and minds of his listeners to understand to whom their worship should be directed.

The true God to be worshipped is He Who has created everything, and Who lives within His whole creation. He certainly 'does not live in shrines made by human hands'. Therefore this God lives within each one of us. Our whole existence is from Him. Until His Son lived in the world, God could overlook the ignorance of men, but now everything has changed through the life, death and Resurrection of the Lord Jesus. There is no longer any excuse for ignorance because this Jesus has revealed to us God's plan, including that of judging the world. It is only through Jesus that there is salvation, and so God commands all people to repent of their ignorances such as worshipping false gods.

However, there were very few Athenians who were moved by Paul's expounding of the true God, 'maker of heaven and earth, and all things seen and unseen, and in one Lord Jesus Christ, His only Son.' It seems that only one member of the Areopagus, Dionysius, was persuaded by Paul's argument, and was one of the few who became Christians in Athens.

The Holy Spirit, the Spirit of Truth whom Jesus has been promising His disciples to send after His Ascension in our readings these past days, can never enter closed hearts and minds. These must always be receptive. St. Basil of Caesarea tells us:

> So the Spirit comes to each of these who receive Him, as though given to him alone; yet He sends out to all His grace, sufficient and complete, and all who partake in Him receive benefit in proportion to the capacity, not of his power, but of their nature.[63]

Thus as we read Paul's experience of preaching to the Athenians, it is a sober reminder for us to ask ourselves on this eve of the Ascension whether our hearts are open to Christ. In a sense our hearts are like the flood gates of a dam: they either are open to admit water or are shut to exclude it. At this Ascensiontide Christ wants us to open our flood gates so that the Spirit can enter because, as He teaches us in today's Gospel, it is only through the Spirit of Truth that we can really come to know Him and the Father. Hilary of Poitiers illustrated this when he wrote:

> Christ dwells in us: and when Christ thus dwells, God dwells. And the Spirit of Christ dwells; and it is not another Spirit than the Spirit of God who dwells. But if Christ is understood to be in us through the Holy Spirit, we must recognize this as both the Spirit of God and the Spirit of Christ.[64]

The Father sends the Holy Spirit through His Son into this world and into us. It is only through the presence of the Spirit that we can have some insight into the meaning of the unity amongst the three Persons within the Godhead which has always existed.

> 'For us there is one God the Father, from whom are all things; and one God the Son through whom are all things; and one Holy Spirit, *in whom are all things.*[65]

So today we are being directed to seek out whether our hearts are indeed like the Athenian altars, so hard that the Spirit of gentleness as well as of might cannot penetrate. In words from the Pentecost Sequence, 'Where thou art not, man has nought'. So let us pray today that the Holy Spirit may 'seek... this soul of mine, And visit it with [His] own ardour glowing.' Then we shall worship the One true God, Lord of all life, and not one of our own idols.

O Ascended Christ, through whom the Spirit is sent, may He fill my heart with His warmth, glow and light, that all stubbornness, aridity, darkness and hardness may be removed. Amen.

[63] H. Bettensen (ed.), *The Later Christian Fathers* (Oxford, 1989), p.71.
[64] Ibid., p.55.
[65] Ibid., p.119.

Ascension Day

The Glorified Lord

To the shout of triumph God has gone up,
the Lord has gone up at the sound of the horn.
Praise God, praise Him with psalms;
praise our King, praise Him with psalms,
for God is King of all the earth.

Psalm 47:5-7

Full readings: Acts 1:1-11; Psalm 47; Ephesians 1:17-23; St. Matthew 28:16-20.

Today is that wonderful day when Our Lord returned to His Father after having wrought our salvation. As we sing in the Ascension Day preface:

Today the Lord Jesus, the king of glory,
the conqueror of sin and death,
ascended to heaven while the angels sang his praises.

In this week's reading Our Lord has been comforting His disciples by assuring them He must return to his Father in order to be with them for ever, 'I will be with you always, to the end of time.' (Mt. 28:20). He will continue to live within us through the Spirit. It is this Spirit that we spoke of yesterday which will enable us to know Christ and His teaching, and which will lead us into all truth.

However, on this Ascension Day as 'He is exalted on high' we realize that Christ has another function. As he is both God and Man He is therefore the Mediator between us and His Father. His Manhood continually pleads for us. 'He has entered heaven . . . to appear now before God on our behalf.' He is 'a priest forever, in the order of Melchizedek'. The writer to the Hebrews tells us, through His Manhood, which was perfected by suffering, 'He became the source of eternal salvation for all who obey Him.' As His priesthood is now perpetual, 'He is able to save completely those who approach God through Him, since He is always alive to plead on their behalf.' Thus, through our eternal High Priest, we can boldly approach the heavenly throne 'in sincerity of heart and the full assurance of faith' (Heb. 5:6, 8-9, 7:25, 9:24, 10:11). If you want to read more about Christ in his function of the eternal priesthood, do read the letters to Hebrews.

It is in the same 'sincerity of heart' that we can also approach the altar day by day. Christ's Manhood unites perpetually the Eucharist with his heavenly oblation. 'The offering of the body of Jesus Christ once for all' was made at Calvary. That can never be repeated, 'Christ, having offered for all time a single sacrifice for sins, took His seat at God's right hand' (Heb. 10:12). Here by God's 'right hand' Christ offers this 'one perfect and sufficient sacrifice' as His heavenly oblation, just as His priest at the altar offers up the one pure sacrifice of Calvary as a commemoration, of which the offering of the bread and wine symbolizes the sacrifice 'of ourselves, souls and bodies'.

The Caroline divine, Jeremy Taylor, when commenting on the uniting of the priest's offering the commemorative sacrifice with Christ's role as the intercessor and mediator in heaven where, as the High Priest, He is still offering 'the same one perfect sacrifice', said:

> For whatsoever Christ did at the institution, the same He commanded the Church to do in remembrance and repeated rites; and Himself also does the same thing in Heaven for us, making perpetual intercession for His Church, the body of His redeemed ones, by representing to His Father His death and Sacrifice. There He sits, a High Priest continually, and offers still the same one perfect sacrifice; that is, still represents it as having been once finished and consummate, in order to perpetual and never-failing events. And this also His ministers do on earth; they offer up the same sacrifice to God, the sacrifice

of the cross, by prayers, and a commemorating rite and representment, according to His Holy institution.[66]

Thus every time we approach the altar we are conscious that heaven and earth are one. As we receive the Lord's Body and Blood we know that we are united with His perpetual sacrifice in heaven where He continually is pleading for us, just as He is continually feeding us while we are still on our earthly pilgrimage.

As we kneel to receive Him on this Ascension Day we honour Him as our King and Majesty who rules over all. 'Seated on His holy throne, God reigns over the nations.' (Ps. 47:9). He is indeed the Sovereign, 'the great King over all the earth'. Before Him we and all creation must bow down and give Him worthy homage as the Ruler of all. As we read in today's Epistle, God 'enthroned Him at His right hand in the heavenly realms, far above all government and authority, all power and dominion, and any title of sovereignty that commands allegiance' (Ep. 1:20-1). In giving His Son this honour the Father has 'put all things in subjection beneath His feet, and gave Him as head over all things to the church' (Ep. 1:22).

On this wonderful feast day, let us as His subjects give our Majesty all that is due unto Him. May our praises and thanks ring out and fill the whole earth, uniting with the choir of heaven as they sing forever of His glory. Let us heed St. Gregory Nazianzen's advice:

> If He ascend up into Heaven ascend with Him. Be one of those angels who escort Him, or one of those who receive Him. Bid the gates be lifted up, or be made higher, exalted after His Passion.[67]

O glorified and ascended Lord, I praise and thank You for Your glorious Ascension because through it You have gone to prepare a place for all your faithful followers, and where You continually plead to the Father on behalf of all mankind. Alleluia! Alleluia! Amen.

---

[66] Taylor, op. cit., Vol. 2, pp.642-3.
[67] St. Gregory Nazianzen, op. cit., p.432.

Friday after the Sixth Sunday of Easter

Joy

'For the moment you are sad; but I shall see you again, and then you will be joyful, and no one will rob you of your joy.'

St. John 16:22

Full readings: Acts 18:9-18; Psalm 47:2-7; St. John 16:20-3.

I am sure we have all experienced that wonderful, overwhelming joy when, for example, a mother meets up again with her son whom she has not seen for a considerable time. The joy which fills her is the kind of joy that Our Lord is speaking of in today's Gospel. When the whole being is engulfed in this well-deep joy, all the sadness of separation vanishes. Jesus warned His disciples they naturally would feel grief at His departure, but that grief would be short-lived and dissipate because they would soon see Him again. Indeed, for the disciples it was not long at all before their Lord and Master was with them again. The joy He promised them they surely experienced, as we have seen as we have followed them from the day of Pentecost. Having received Christ through His Spirit they immediately began preaching the Gospel until this Apostolic Church had touched nearly every part of the Roman empire.

The lives of the early Christians were indeed lives full of joy because they knew that Jesus was with them. Silas and Paul's hymns of praise in prison were the outward expression of the inward joy they felt for being able to suffer for their Lord. So many of the early saints gladly faced death rather than deny their God. Polycarp, for instance, when asked to take the oath before the proconsul and 'swear by the Fortune of Caesar', uttered those words which have become famous: 'For six and eighty years I have been serving Him, and He has done no wrong to me, how, then, dare I blaspheme my King who has saved me!' For his denial of Caesar, Polycarp was sentenced to die at the stake. This the old saint dismissed as nothing. After all, 'the fire which you threaten is one that burns for a little while, and after a short time goes out', but the fires of hell last forever. Indeed, the stake was Polycarp's joy, reflected in this prayer he offered once bound:

> I bless You because You have seen fit to bestow upon me this day and this hour, that I may share, among the number of the martyrs, the cup of Your Anointed and to rise to eternal life both in soul and body, in virtue of the immortality of the Holy Spirit. May I be accepted among them in your sight today as a rich and pleasing sacrifice, such as You, the true God who cannot utter a false-hood, has prearranged, revealed in advance and now consummated.[68]

The joy experienced by Polycarp can be ours too because Jesus is also saying to us that, through His very presence in the living Spirit, we too can have joy. Easter we know is a period of wonderful joy, and our lives do abound in radiancy from the sheer joy of celebrating so many blessings from our celebrating the Resurrection after the self-denial, prayer and fasting of Lent and Holy Week. Yet what we celebrate during the great Fifty Days should spill over for the rest of the year too. The mere fact that Jesus is always with us means joy in our lives; the fact that we may experience something of the beauty and holiness of eternal life now is joy; and the fact that we shall live with our dear Saviour forever amongst all the angels and saints is joy. Of all peoples Christians should be the most joyful because there is nothing else in life that gives the same joy of knowing we have a Saviour. This Saviour, who absorbed all our sins into His dying body, then conquered death so that we could be freed from the slavery of sin. All we have to do, as the disciples told their auditors over and over again, is to repent of our sins and be baptized. What news of joy, no wonder it is often referred to as the *Good News*:

When will you come, Jesus my Joy, to save me from care, and give Yourself to me, that I may see You evermore?

Could I but come to You, all my desires were fulfilled! I seek nothing but You alone, Who is all my desire.

Jesus my Saviour! Jesus my Comforter! Flower of all beauty!

My help and my succour! When may I see You in Your majesty?[69]

So let our lives experience that joy which Jesus not only promised but gives, and is! 'Jesus, my Hope, my Salvation, my only Joy!'[70]

O Ascended Lord, You have assured me, through the sending of the Spirit, You are always present; may I rejoice in knowing You are closer to me than even my own breathing. You are my joy, my delight, my inspiration, my strength and my defence. All praise and honour be Yours, O Holy Son of God. Amen.

[68] St. Polycarp, op. cit., pp.94-5, 97.
[69] R. Rolle, *Selected Works of Richard Rolle*, ed. G.C. Heseltine (London, 1930), p.98.
[70] Ibid.

Saturday after the Sixth Sunday of Easter

The Father

'In very truth I tell you, if you ask the Father for anything
in my name, He will give it you. So far you have asked
nothing in my name. Ask and you will receive, that your
joy may be complete.'

St. John 16:23-4

Full readings: Acts 18:23-8; Psalm 47:2-3, 8-10; St. John 16:23-8.

Not only will the disciples have joy through Jesus' return, but they
have also been assured that when they ask for anything in 'my name' it
will be granted to them by the Father. 'Ask and you will receive.' As we
know only too well from our reading of Acts, this is precisely what
happened as they ministered amongst the various churches. In 'the
name of Jesus' the lame walked, the sick were healed, the pagans
converted, and even the dead restored to life. It was because the
apostles were seemingly working miracles in this Name that the various
authorities tried to silence them, and prevent them doing anything
more in the name of Jesus. Sometimes the opposition to their preaching
and healings was through jealousy, as seems to be the case in today's
reading from Acts when the Jews in Corinth brought Paul before the
courts. Sometimes the opposition was through greed, as in the case of
the slave masters in Philippi. Nevertheless, irrespective of what kind of
opposition, punishment and imprisonment the apostles met, it could
not stop the work of God being done in the name of Jesus because this
was the will of the Father.

In the Church of the twentieth century this teaching of Jesus, to ask in 'my name' and the Father will grant it, has diminished. Is this because the Church has over-valued the material things at the expense of the spiritual? Or have we simply forgotten how to ask? Although we know that our heavenly Father knows all our needs before we ask, nevertheless He wants us to approach Him for our daily needs. To ask Our Father through Christ for our physical and spiritual wants and healings implies that we must also believe that He will give them. This was the wonderful thing about the early Church; the apostles and saints boldly believed that what they were asking for in Christ's name would be given. They knew the sheer power of invoking the name of Jesus. That is the name that no evil can withstand, and that is why, when Paul commanded 'in the name of Jesus Christ' for the evil spirit to come out of the slave girl, it did. We too must believe in the power of that most holy Name in healing, cleansing, reconciling and restoring all kinds of situations in this world. It will only be through Christ's name that those who live irreconcilably will be reconciled; those who live in hatred will learn to love; those who cannot forgive will be able to forgive; those who cannot repent of sins will taste the pure joy of release from sin. Sometimes when we approach God for a need we tend to think only in terms of healing someone's illness, and never realize that there are more important things for God to heal than physical pain. Reconciliation indeed means coming to grips with Satan and all kinds of evil. Indeed, so often physical healing cannot take place until spiritual healings occur, that is, until there is true reconciliation within people. After all, physical pain won't ever kill the soul, but hatred, jealousy, bitterness, anger and revenge will. Thus a regular part of our daily intercessions should be asking the Father in Jesus' name for spiritual healing of all those who need it so desperately, until they can say, like the gaoler, 'What must I do to be saved?' Then and then only will reconciliation and healing begin to break through this sorry world of so much hatred and violence.

Indeed, this prayer from the Corrymeela Community may assist any who are not sure about commitment to asking the Father through the Son for reconciliation and healing to take place in the hearts possessed by evil at present:

> God, we believe that You have called us together to broaden our experience of You and of each other.

We believe that we have been called to help in healing the many wounds of society and in reconciling man to man and man to God.
Help us, as individuals or together, to work, in love, for peace, and never to lose heart.
We commit ourselves to each other–in joy and sorrow.
We commit ourselves to all who share our belief in reconciliation– to support and stand by them.
We commit ourselves to You–as our guide and friend.[71]

O holy Jesu, the name above every other name, let me firmly believe that when I petition the Father through You, the Father will grant my prayer. Cast away any doubts I may have, and let me trust in your power to heal and reconcile all kinds of brokenness and sickness in this world. Amen.

[71] The Corrymeela Community, based in Belfast in Northern Ireland, is a fellowship of Christians from different religious backgrounds bound together with an ardent desire to work and pray for the reconciliation of all Irishmen, and for all other people in the world where peace and unity are desperately needed.

The Seventh Sunday of Easter

Glory

'I have glorified You on earth by finishing the work which
You gave me to do; and now, Father, glorify me in Your
own presence with the glory which I had with You before
the world began.'

St. John 17:4-5

Full readings: Acts 1:12-14; Psalm 27; 1 Peter 4:13-16; St. John
17:1-11.

Today's Gospel comes from what we know as the High Priestly
prayer offered by Jesus to His Father before Gethesemane. In it we see
the perfect obedience of the Son to the Father in fulfilling His will. In
order to fulfil the Father's will, the Son had to leave His home, but now
as that is fulfilled it is time for the Son to return. What was the fulfilling
of that will? To proclaim the Lord as Sovereign over all the earth, to
reveal the Father to all through the Son, and to teach the Father's
commands. This early Syriac liturgy illustrates the relationship between
the Father and Son:

> Jesus Christ, radiant centre of glory,
> image of our God, the invisible Father,
> revealer of His eternal designs,
> Prince of peace;
> Father of the world to come.[72]

In accomplishing all of these, the Son glorified the Father because by Himself He could do nothing. The Father worked through His Son for redeeming the world, as the Father and Son are One. Now all that is finished, it is time to go home; it is time for the Son to be glorified in heaven now that 'man's redeeming work has been done'. It is really a matter of the Son assuming once again that glory He has had since before the world began, but which He had temporarily laid aside.

Apart from grasping the unison of the Father and Son, in which the Son glorifies the Father, and the Father the Son, the other important teaching for us is the availability of eternal life, the life that the Father wishes for us, through the Son. 'I have come that they may have life, and may have it in all its fullness.' (Jn. 10:10). To share in this eternal life with the Father and Son, all that is necessary for us is to know the Father, 'the only true God, and Jesus Christ whom you have sent' (Jn. 17:3). Thus all the teachings of Jesus are consummated in knowing the Father through His Son. When Jesus told His disciples that He was going home to His Father whom they also knew, Philip replied, 'Lord, show us the Father.' How discouraging this was for Jesus is illustrated in His answer, 'Have I been all this time with you, Philip, and still you do not know me? Anyone who has seen me has seen the Father.' (Jn. 14:7-9).

Eternal life we know begins here with Baptism; it is not something which we hanker after in the future. Yet we can only have this eternal, this abundant life through our relationship with the 'true God'. We all surely know we can only have a lively and living relationship with someone after we get to know a person. It is never achieved when we make our first acquaintance. The more effort we make to know what a person is really like the easier it is to build on that first acquaintance until we can honestly say we have established a relationship of some worth.

Thus for us who desire more than anything else to live in the now with Him Who gives life to the full, we have to spend time, and more time in getting to know more about Him. It means reading and meditating on the Gospels each day; there is always something afresh to see each time we ponder on them. That is one of the joys of the Gospel news–these new discoveries and enlightenments, as I have been finding in writing this series of meditations. And we can never separate our reading of the Gospels from prayer. Our meditations, if meaningfully undertaken, invariably begin with, and end in prayer. We seek the

Spirit of all knowledge to unveil to us new understandings of and encounters with Christ. Perhaps we may find helpful St. Francis' paraphrase of the petition 'Hallowed be Thy name' from the Lord's Prayer:

> May Your knowledge shine in us, that we may know the breadth of Your benefits, the length of Your promises, the height of Your majesty, and the depth of Your judgments.[73]

From the Epistle for today we learn how important it is for us to glorify the 'true God' in our daily lives. Just as the Son glorified the Father in His earthly work, so must He be glorified through us in what we are and do, and in any suffering we endure. The whole world should be unceasingly glorifying the Father. His glory will be manifest when we humbly bow to God's will in our lives, and when we no longer are always seeking to glorify ourselves in doing our will. The more we learn to say 'yes' to God, and 'no' to ourselves, the more His glory will shine in His world.

You only are worthy to receive praise and glory, and honour and blessing O Father. Just as the Son glorifies You, teach me to glorify You also in all that I am and do, dear Father, by carrying out Your will. Amen.

[72] Berselli, op. cit., p.32.
[73] St. Francis of Assisi, op. cit., p.170.

Monday after the Seventh Sunday of Easter

The Conqueror

'I have told you all this so that in me you may find peace.
In the world you will have suffering. But take heart! I
have conquered the world.'

St. John 16:33

Full readings: Acts 19:1-8; Psalm 68:2-7; St. John 16:29-33.

Before His Passion not only does Our Lord promise His disciples
that He will be always with them, even though He must leave them, but
He also assures them that nothing which they will face in life will be too
difficult for them, nor any suffering be too great because He has
'conquered the world'. Through Him they will always have victory over
all kinds of corruption, even the darkest deeds of men. Jesus gives them
this wonderful encouragement because He realized that, just as He had
been plotted against, reviled and hated for doing the Father's will, so
will be His disciples when they preach in His name.

The disciples in due course discovered how true this was once they
began carrying out Our Lord's command to 'go . . . to all nations and
make them my disciples; baptize them in the name of the Father and
the Son and the Holy Spirit, and teach them to observe all that I have
commanded you.' (Mt. 28:19-20). During these great Fifty Days we
have read many times of their physical sufferings through their preaching, healing and baptizing. Yet they continue to move from province to
province, town to town, fearless in doing the Lord's work. They 'are
joyful, they exalt before God with gladness and rejoicing' (Ps. 68:3) in

any kind of physical punishment and persecution.

In the assurance that Christ has conquered the world, the disciples toiled unceasingly, and consequently the number of Christians increased daily. In today's lesson we have another example of this when Paul at Ephesus baptized 'about a dozen men in all' with the Holy Spirit. Previously these men had known only the baptism of repentance through John. Now the receiving of the Holy Spirit makes them new men, and was manifested in them by speaking in tongues.

Jesus, in conquering the world, is also 'our refuge, and our stronghold, a timely help in trouble' (Ps. 46:1). We too can be assured that this world's 'mightiest powers have done their worst' to Christ who has overcome them all, and therefore there is nothing worse left for us ever to face. As Christ has conquered the worst in this world, we can also in His name. We can triumph over and absorb every bit of suffering, hatred, spite, ambition and rejection which comes our way. We can also cope with all the problems and tensions of work, at home and personal relationships through Our Lord. He always gives us the means if we but seek them.

The other important fact from today's Gospel is that at long last the disciples as a whole began to see their Lord and Master for whom He really is. They begin to comprehend His relationship with His Father, from whom He came into this world, and that in knowing Him they were also learning about God the Father. Nevertheless, it was not until Pentecost that they fully understood their Master's mission. They needed the Spirit of Truth to enable them to know Truth completely.

Before we can accept unquestionably that Jesus has 'conquered the world', we too must be able to say, 'we believe that You have come from God' and 'that You know everything' (Jn. 16:30). As we prepare this week to celebrate Pentecost, when the Holy Spirit was poured out upon the Church, let us pray that we shall be blessed with many, many gifts of the Spirit, especially that of faith. Our Lord Himself stressed how important faith is in our acknowledging Him as Lord of this world, and accepting His teaching. We know when everything seems against us, it is hard not to be dejected and discouraged, and the fact that Jesus has been there does not seem to comfort us at all. So we need to pray fervently that we shall receive faith, faith sufficient to say, 'Lord I do believe'; and through that to accept that, in every situation we face, Christ is indeed there. There is absolutely nothing which He cannot share with us in our times of darkness, despair, grief, agony and uncertainty. However, sometimes Our Lord does not appear to make Himself known in this sharing, and that is why we need faith, this most precious gift. It is only our faith which will enable us to accept that Jesus has conquered this world, and therefore there is nothing to fear or worry about. He is with us. St. Paul in his letter to the Romans assures us of this when he declares:

What can separate us from the love of Christ? Can affliction or hardship? Can persecution, hunger, nakedness, danger or sword? . . . Throughout it all, overwhelming victory is ours through Him who loved us. . . . For I am convinced there is nothing . . . in all creation that can separate us from the love of God in Christ Jesus Our Lord.

(Rom. 8:35-9)

O blessed Spirit, pour Your gifts upon me, especially that of faith, so that I may believe that Our Lord has conquered all this world's darkest deeds, and therefore there is nothing for me to fear. You are indeed my 'refuge and stronghold, a very present help in trouble'. Amen.

Tuesday after the Seventh Sunday of Easter

The Third Missionary Journey

'All I want is to finish the race, and complete the task which the Lord Jesus assigned me, that of bearing my testimony to the gospel of God's grace.'

Acts 20:24

Full readings: Acts 20:17-27; Psalm 68:10-11, 20-1; St. John 17:1-11.

During his third journey the Holy Spirit made known to Paul that it would be no easy time for him as 'in city after city . . . imprisonment and hardships' awaited him (Acts 20:23). What the Spirit is prophesying to Paul is what we heard Jesus tell His disciples in yesterday's Gospel, that they would indeed face many sufferings in His name. It was also made clear to Paul that, once he departed from the Asian churches, there would be 'savage wolves' who would enter and try to devour the many flocks he had built up. Indeed, some of these 'wolves' would come from within and scatter Christians!

Hence there is a sense of urgency in Paul's work now, in order to complete the task that the Lord Jesus had given him. That task had been to proclaim the kingdom, and to disclose wherever he preached, 'the whole purpose of God'. As we learn from today's Gospel, we know that purpose was to teach the meaning of eternal life, and to proclaim God's sovereignty over this world.

Sunday's reading for the Gospel was the same as today's, and we discovered then that eternal life comes from acknowledging the Father and His Son Jesus Christ as true God. This is what Paul taught 'in public and in ... homes' to both Jew and Gentile unceasingly throughout Asia Minor.

Paul in preaching on eternal life could teach about it so fervently through his own dramatic experience on the road to Damascus. Thus he expounded how it begins with 'repentance before God and faith in Our Lord Jesus'. And to continue experiencing eternal life involves repeated repentance and faith. Today, as we continue our preparation for Pentecost, let us continue to pray to be given the Spirit of Truth so that we can recognize the many ways we fail God, our neighbour and ourselves. Each day we commit sins of omission as well as those of commission. As sin separates us from God and from one another, we should be able to see the sheer necessity of repentance in our daily lives if we wish to stay within the kingdom of heaven. Therefore 'every single sin which we remember must be repented of by an act of repentance that must particularly touch that sin.' We can never believe that 'one act of sorrow can abolish many foul acts of sin'; if we do 'we deceive ourselves'.[74] Our daily examination, guided by the Holy Spirit, will help us to be aware of those besetting sins. Once we recognize that we do have besetting sins, the next step is to overcome them through the living Spirit. We can never overcome them if we try to do so by our own efforts. It is only through Christ's living presence that we can make progress. If we are not making any progress at all, it is an S.O.S., telling us that we are not seeking divine help. Jeremy Taylor stressed the importance of 'speedily' repenting if we desire to attain a more Christ-centred life:

> ... it being impossible to live innocently, it is necessary that a way of God's own finding out should be relied upon ... And though I sin, yet I repent speedily, and when I sin again I repent again, and my spiritual state is like my natural, day and night succeed each other by a never-failing revolution. I sin indeed in some instances, but I do my duty in many; and every man has his infirmities; no man can say: 'My soul is pure from sin,' but I hope that because I repent still as I sin, my sins are but as a single action; and since I resist them when I can, I hope they will be reckoned to me but as sins of infirmity, without which no man is or can be in this state of perfection.[75]

We also need faith, which I touched on yesterday. This faith is in Christ who we believe has given us this eternal life. This faith should not be a mere flicker but a burning fire within us. It is also meant to be a lively faith. What else should it be when we have been assured that Christ has triumphed over death, and now lives in glory with His Father where He prepares to welcome us? Through Christ is life, an abundancy of life and a new life! This is what is meant by eternal life now. It is there for every person to enjoy, and the gateway is what Paul preached all through that hazardous third missionary journey, repentance and faith.

O Holy Spirit, fill me with truth, so that I may see my sins as You see them, and then give me sufficient grace to repent of them, and then strength to overcome them. Fill me also with a lively faith in Christ, so that I may enjoy eternal life now. Amen.

[74] Taylor, op. cit., Vol.7, p.180.
[75] Ibid., Vol. 7, p.11.

Wednesday after the Seventh Sunday of Easter

Giving

All along I showed you that it is our duty to help the weak
in this way, by hard work, and that we should keep in
mind the words of the Lord Jesus, who himself said,
'Happiness lies more in giving than receiving.'

Acts 20:35

Full readings: Acts 20:28-38; Psalm 68:29-30, 33-6; St. John 17:11-19.

We probably know the Authorized Version 'It is more blessed to give
that to receive' better than the above translation. Yet both are saying
the same: we become richer in spirit when we give to others than when
we receive. These are Paul's parting words to the church at Miletus. He
urges them to be sensitive to the needs of their brethren, and wherever
they find help needed, to give it, and to give it most generously.

Ever since his conversion on the road to Damascus, Paul was tireless
in his own giving, giving without ever counting the cost of toil in his
ministry to the various churches he helped to establish. Never was his
giving more prominent than it was when he said his sad farewells on the
Milesian waterfront to the local Christians. Sad for Paul because he
knew that many of these Christians would be like lambs amongst
wolves which would ravage so much of his teaching, and sad also for the
local congregation as Paul informed them they would never see him
again.

St. Paul's giving unstintingly was modelled on Christ. As Christ gave
so did he and so should we in return for His gifts. It is precisely because

God gave first, that we can in fact give anything at all.

In St. Matthew's Gospel we are told because we receive freely, we must give accordingly (Mt. 10:8). In many ways it is much easier to give to another person than to receive a gift. We have all met those people who always want to pay the bill after a meal, and somehow I feel that has very little to do with the kind of giving Jesus and Paul were teaching about and exemplifying in their lives.

To be blessed in giving means that giving must cost the giver something. That is why Our Lord commended the poor widow for her giving of two tiny coins to the temple's treasury rather than the gifts of the rich people. Her giving cost her all, while the rich gave only in a token way (Lk. 21:2). It is so easy to give our left-overs to a poor family, but is that real giving? Would we use them for ourselves? What we have to learn as Christians is to share some of our possessions which mean something to us; something we don't really want to part with. When we do we shall discover how much blessedness there is in giving. This is the kind of giving God gives. The Incarnation is surely God sharing and giving of His cream. When we reflect on Christ's birth we are struck, almost dumbfounded, that God, the Almighty, would 'condescend to be born as children are born; [and] to become a Child.' The Omnipotent One 'who thunders in heaven', should cry in a cradle. The One 'who is so great and so high, should become so little as a child, and so low as a manger.' And the Omniscient One should 'not...abhor the Virgin's womb, not...abhor the beasts' manger, [and] not...disdain to be fed with butter and honey.'[76]

The Nativity is but the beginning of God's giving. This week we have been reflecting upon Our Lord having accomplished all that His Father desired. To fulfil the will of His Father also included the bitter cup in the garden, and the horrible, degrading spectacle at Golgotha where the broken Body of Christ is sneered at by onlookers. Yes, this is the cost of God's giving. But it did not stop at Golgotha. It continues and continues and will continue until the end of the world. Before Gethesemane He gave us the gift of Himself, a living gift in the Bread which He broke and the Cup which He blessed. And now at Pentecost He gives us His abiding presence through the Spirit. How abundantly we have received from Our God, and at great cost to Him. In giving Himself to us, He has shown us what is meant by giving.

For us to give abundantly it first means that we have to receive. We have to receive the gifts of the Spirit in order to give to others. This in turn teaches us another truth about giving. It means not only giving of our possessions, but giving of our Christian virtues. We all meet situations every day where we need to give patience rather than impatience; humility rather than arrogance; compassion rather than contempt; listening rather than talking; acceptance rather than judgment and, above all, love instead of hate. When we learn to give truly of the virtues of the kingdom of heaven we enter another level of giving. It is that kind of giving that makes us what Christ calls us in today's Gospel, 'strangers in this world'. Spiritual giving is a very rare thing, but so many people need to receive it. Only a couple of days ago, when I was visiting a retired priest who has Parkinson's disease in a nursing home, he remarked to me, 'What I miss most is receiving spiritual gifts from my visitors.' He needs them, and so do many, many others.

This Pentecost let us pray earnestly that we share our spiritual gifts with others, and never to be afraid of, or feel awkward about it. If we live in the Spirit, then it is as natural to want to feed the soul as it is to feed the physical hunger of a person.

O Holy Spirit, fill me with Your many gifts, and then let me in turn give the fruits of these to all I meet. Make me generous in giving of time, self, spiritual values and worldly possessions to others. Amen.

[76] Andrewes, op. cit., Vol. 1, p.29.

Thursday after the Seventh Sunday of Easter

Unity

'I in them and You in me, may they be perfectly one. Then the world will know that You sent me, and that You loved them as You loved me.'

St. John 17:23

Full readings: Acts 22:30, 23:6-11; Psalm 16:1-2, 5-7, 7-11; St. John 17:20-6.

Our Blessed Lord had repeatedly stressed the unity between Himself as Son and His Father, they are one in all things. It is this unity which He earnestly desires for His Church, and prays that all members may be one. Indeed, Jesus is teaching us that this unity is essential if the world is going to know that the Son has been sent by the Father into this world to reveal Him and His teaching. Furthermore, if the Father is going to be glorified, once again oneness amongst all believers is imperative.

How it must break the Sacred Heart of Jesus to see how much disunity there is amongst the churches, and horror, oh, horror, that Christians kill one another in the name of their religion! Did Our Saviour die on the Cross so degradingly to redeem all mankind, and to give them abundant life, to have man stoop to so much bigotry, hatred, squabbling over doctrines, and denying fellow Christians His Life in the Blessed Sacrament? Where there is love, there is God. If we truly possess love, then we yearn with all our hearts, minds and souls for all to be at one in Him. Therefore it is essential that, as we approach this celebrating of Pentecost, we pray for the gift of love, and that love may always abide in us. The English mystic, Walter Hilton, described this so well when he insisted that this gift of Divine Love makes perfect peace between God and a soul, and unites all blessed creatures wholly in God. This is the bond of Divine Love which unites Jesus to us, and us to Him, and enables us 'to love one another in Him.'[77] I am convinced that if we strove to possess this love then all disunity amongst Christians would disappear, and we all would be truly one in the Breaking of the Bread.

When I pray for the healing of Christ's Body, the Church, every day, I so often think how would we like our own bodies to be broken over, over and over again for the same thing? Why is it we seem to want to perpetuate this brokenness of Christ's Body? When we are baptized we are made 'members of Christ' and also 'inheritors of the kingdom of heaven'. Surely we do not believe that on Judgment Day we shall be judged on doctrine, but whether we indeed have loved in its fullest sense. It will be Love who will bring us to heaven, and it will be Love dwelling within us who will guide us there.

Thank God there are many Christians today who are firmly committed to work towards the healing of Christ's broken Body. By that I mean they pray earnestly each day for it, and live it out in their communications and worshipping with fellow Christians. This is a genuine attempt by Christians who see themselves utmostly as Christians and not as a Catholic or Methodist or Lutheran. They give far more than the cosmetic approach that many of the main churches do. I have often thought how pathetic is the Church's intent for unity even during the so-called Week of Christian Unity, mostly held in January in the northern hemisphere. Can a choir exchanging churches do all that much towards achieving the unity that Christ demands? Having lived in Australia for most of my life, I always thought the time for earnest prayer for Christian unity was more appropriate, that is, at this time of the year where the days between the Ascension and Pentecost are kept as a Novena for the healing of all kinds of division amongst Christians. Certainly during this time, the readings are far more conducive to thinking about what Christ taught about unity and what St. Paul meant by being One in Christ.

Nevertheless, after saying that I do know, and thank God for it, there have been great advances made in ecumenical dialogue since Vatican Two. But from the bottom of my heart I believe if we truly want

Christ's Body to be one as it is meant to be, then it would happen. How awful it is to see Catholics–Roman and Anglican–having to communicate at different parts of a church! At this present moment in time when we think of unity it means more the pain we experience of not being able to receive the Sacrament at the same altar. O blessed will be that day when we can receive the Body and Blood of Christ kneeling beside one another. When will we humbly confess our sin and sorrow for disunity and perpetuating this brokenness of Christ's Body? When are we going to seek healing through Christ's power to remove all our divisions? When are we going to take Our Lord's words seriously that 'they all be one'? Or St. Paul's, based on his Lord's:

> We are to maintain the truth in a spirit of love; so we shall fully grow up into Christ. He is the head, and on Him the whole body depends. Bonded and held together by every constituent joint, the whole flame grows through the proper functioning of each part, and build itself up in love.
>
> (Eph. 4:15-16)

Indeed, the readings for Pentecost stress the unity of all in Christ's Body through the Spirit. St. Paul again reminds us that, although we shall all receive different gifts at Pentecost, nevertheless they all come from the one and the same Spirit. These individual gifts are like the 'limbs and organs' which 'make up one body', the Body of Christ. Into this Body we are brought by the Spirit to be baptized, irrespective of race or class, and though this Body has many organs it is still one Body. By virtue of our baptism we are all made one in Christ, not many who are divided and argue over this Body (1 Cor. 14).

Thus in our preparations for Pentecost let us remember that it is Jesus' earnest will that we are one Body. There is only one Faith and one Shepherd who calls us to love one another as He loves us. He is calling us committed Christians to work for this to happen. If we ardently seek His gift of Love, it will open and enlighten us to know truth. That truth is that God Incarnate not only gives His Life daily to us at the Eucharist, but gave us His Life at Calvary, and now He implores us to be one as He and His Father are One.

O Blessed Spirit, so fill me with love and truth that I may seek with all my being the healing of fragmentation amongst Christians in the knowledge that You pray, and longingly desire for all Your children to be one in You who died, rose from death and ascended in all glory. Amen.

[77] W. Hilton, *The Scale of Perfection* (London, 1901), p.255.

Friday after the Seventh Sunday of Easter

The Trials of Paul

'But Paul appealed to be remanded in custody for his imperial majesty's decision, and I [i.e. Festus] ordered him to be detained until I could send him to the emperor.'

Acts 25:21

Full readings: Acts 25:13-21; Psalm 103:1-2, 11-12, 19- 20; St. John 21:15-19.

Paul had returned to Jerusalem. James, who was aware of the local Jewish animosity towards Paul, advised him to take the four Jewish Christians who were living under a vow there into the temple for a week to undergo the ritual of purification, in order to show that he himself was still quite prepared to observe the laws of Moses. This, James hoped, would appease the Jews. However, it did not appease all of them, and Jews from Asia, after seeing Paul in the temple, brought the city to a tumult over Paul's teaching. Thus began that long period of trials as well as many tribulations for Paul before he eventually reached Rome as he had appealed to the emperor to hear his case.

In today's lesson we find Paul in Caesarea where he had been sent by the Roman authorities in order to escape the Jewish plot to lynch him. After his initial trial there before Felix, the Roman Governor had dismissed the Jewish religious authorities' case against Paul. Here he subsequently remained in open prison for two years until a new Governor, Festus, arrived who wanted to court favour with the Jews. This he proposed to do by sending Paul back to Jerusalem for trial.

Upon hearing this, Paul, by using his rights as a Roman citizen, appealed to be heard by Caesar himself. While Felix was still in Caesarea, King Agrippa and his wife arrived and were intrigued about Paul's presence, and enquired whether they might converse with him. Thus once again Paul pours out his account of conversion and his obedience to 'the heavenly vision'. So enthusiastic is he for all to know the joy which comes from believing in Christ, he blurts out to Agrippa, 'I wish to God that not only you, but all those who are listening to me today, might become what I am – apart from these chains!' (Acts 26:29). Indeed, we can almost hear Paul, despite his chains, giving thanks to His God for all His blessings in the words of today's Psalm:

Bless the Lord, my soul;
with all my being I bless His holy name.
Bless the Lord, my soul,
and forget none of His benefits.
He pardons all my wrong doing
and heals all my ills.
He rescues me from death's pit
and crowns me with love and compassion.

(Ps. 103:1-4)

In today's Gospel we hear for the second time during these Fifty Days the account of Jesus before His Ascension asking Peter whether he indeed loves Him above everything else. From the very bottom of his heart Peter tells his Lord that indeed he loves Him, and adds a caveat, 'You know everything; You know I love You' (Jn. 21:17), to strengthen his sincerity and his future resolve. What Peter said could easily have been said by Paul. Paul who had persecuted Jesus, his Lord, over and over again, many more times than the three denials by Peter, had therefore been forgiven much. Consequently he laboured more than any other disciple to preach the redeeming Love of Christ. That labour had brought him imprisonment, scourging, stoning, beatings, shipwreck, and all kinds of dangers from travelling while preaching. He also had endured sleeplessness, hunger, thirst, cold and exposure. But the hardest to endure was the unfaithfulness of Christians to their Lord and their jealousy and hatred towards one another (2 Cor. 5:16 ff., 6:*passim*, 11:23 ff., 1 Cor. 2:3-4). Yet all these he gladly suffered for Christ whose Love shone through Paul's ministry.

So just as Our Lord challenged Peter and Paul with the question, 'Do you love me?', so He is also challenging us with exactly the same question. Yet to love God is not something we can do in our own strength; it is the gift of the Spirit for which we must be constantly asking. We shall know we possess Divine Love through the quality of our living because this love 'slays mightily anger and envy, and all passions of wrath and melancholy in it and brings into the soul the virtues of patience and mildness, peaceableness and amity to his neighbour.' By possessing such love we no longer 'strive and fight and plead for earthly goods' as we are content with what we have. We desire 'no more of all the riches on earth than a scanty bodily sustenance for to sustain [our] bodily life.'[78] Pentecost is the feast of Love. Let us not lose sight of that as we draw very near to our keeping of it.

> Love for ever dwells in Heaven,
>   Hope entereth not there.
> To despairing man Love's given,
>   Hope dwelleth not with despair.
> Love reigneth high, and reigneth low,
>   and reigneth everywhere.[79]

O Blessed Spirit, fill me with love divine until it consumes my whole being, and sets me on fire to preach, toil and suffer as Paul and Peter did. Give me an unquenchable desire to be faithful to You until the end. Amen.

[78] Hilton, op. cit., pp.264, 268.
[79] Rossetti, op. cit., p.83.

Saturday after the Seventh Sunday of Easter

The Vigil of Pentecost

TESTIMONY

It is the same disciple who vouches for what has been written here. He it is who wrote it, and we know that his testimony is true.

St. John 21:24

Full readings: Acts 28:16-20, 30-1; Psalm 11:4-5, 7; St. John 21:20-5.

As the great Fifty Days draw to a close we come to the end of our readings from Acts and St. John's Gospel. I always get a tremendous thrill from reading these together. This Gospel is for me the most wonderful piece of literature ever written as it unfolds 'the great Mystery'. The Word became flesh and dwelt amongst us as the will and work of the Father was accomplished through His Son. It is full of mysticism, rich in life in the Spirit, and the unity of the Godhead. It is also the fruits of a Church living out the Gospel before it was written by St. John or one of his disciples. Acts is St. Luke's account of the early Church in living out the teachings of the Risen and Ascended Lord as expressed in this Gospel. Both witness that what Our Lord taught was true. He indeed is 'the Way, the Life and the Truth'. Both show clearly that only Jesus could give eternal life, and that was God's purpose for becoming Man. In Christ was also revealed the Father so that all who believed would know God. Both reveal that, although God offers eternal life to all, there are many who shun Truth and Light because they prefer their own darkness, and therefore will never taste eternal delights. Christ came to dismantle darkness so that all may be bathed in His glorious Light. Both exclaim that freedom is the passport of being a Christian because through Baptism the believer is freed from the tyranny of sin, the world and flesh, and arises a new, liberated person in Christ.

Acts finishes with Paul in Rome, the pulse of the Roman world, to await his appeal to Caesar. He was allowed private lodgings with a police escort. In such a free environment he was able to expound 'from dawn to dusk' the meaning of the Scriptures to the many visitors he had. As Paul, unhindered in Rome, explained the Scriptures with its fulfilling in Christ, I am reminded of another great Father of the early Church, St. Ambrose, who lived not far away in Milan in the fourth century and who also spent his days expounding the Scriptures. One day a rather arrogant, polished rhetorician came to listen to him. That listening changed his life, and the course of much Western theology! In A.D. 387 St. Augustine was baptized during the Easter Vigil Liturgy after his Lenten course of preparation under the guidance of the great St. Ambrose.

St. John's Gospel ends with that wonderful challenge as we saw yesterday to Peter by Our Lord, and today it concludes with the prophesying of Peter's martyrdom. Those two spearheads in the early Church, Peter and Paul, tradition tells us died under the great persecution of Nero c. A.D. 64. Their martyrdom we commemorate on the 29th of June each year. However, the Gospel does not end right there. It continues with a few more but powerful verses. In the first of these the author assures us that everything which has been disclosed is true: 'his testimony is true'; and the other is the acknowledgement that what has been recorded is but a portion of everything that Jesus did, so numerous were these that one would run out of books to contain them, thus unfolding how abundantly generous the God who became incarnate to bring us salvation is. What a wonderful way to end these Fifty Days, to ponder on how many yet more marvellous things we shall discover in our heavenly home.

And now to the Vigil of the Pentecost; our thoughts must turn to this great feast and proper preparation for it. Pentecost, the old Jewish festival of giving the first fruits of the harvest to God, now superseded by Christ being the first fruit 'of His creation' (Jam. 1:18), and 'of the harvest of the dead'. Our Lord is the first fruit of life, and through that is our hope. Just as Jesus, the unblemished lamb, offered His life to God and the Jews offered to God their first fruits of the earth, so must we offer our first fruits. It may also be helpful for us to recall that when the Jews made their gifts they also recited a thanksgiving of how the Lord had been merciful and kind to them in delivering them from their bondage in Egypt and bringing them to 'a land with wheat and barley, vines, fig trees, and pomegranates, a land with olive oil and honey.' (Deut. 8:8). As we bring our first fruits, that is the best of what we have and are to the altar, let us also do it in thanksgiving for the bondage from which Christ has delivered us, and for the promised land to which He had brought us, a land indeed 'flowing with olive oil and honey'. Oh, how many are the gifts He gives us through the Spirit! All this week we have prayed about receiving various gifts of the Spirit, notably those of faith, truth, understanding and love. When we receive the gifts of the Spirit we are then able to manifest in our lives the fruits of the Spirit of which above all else is love. Apart from love there are those other virtues which Paul enumerated for us: 'joy, peace, patience, kindness, goodness, fidelity, gentleness and self-control' (Gal. 5:22). How different are these from the behaviour of those not living in the Spirit of Christ. St. Paul tells us that these people manifest 'fornication, indecency, and debauchery; idolatry and sorcery, quarrels, a contentious temper, envy, fits of rage, selfish ambitions, dissensions, party intrigues, and jealousies; drinking bouts, orgies and the like' (Gal. 5:19-20). When we see them juxtapositioned it hits home, doesn't it, just how different is the living in the Spirit of Christ as against the world's? That is why Our Lord warned us that the world would never understand His coming nor His teaching. Let us pray that we may always understand that we must show forth the fruits of the Spirit in our lives.

In our preparation for the feast of gifts we cannot overlook that other Testimony which St. John's Gospel unfolds. 'He will bear witness to me' (Jn. 15:26). The Spirit of Truth will testify to the whole world 'of Christ, that He is God, that He is man, that He is Christ, the Saviour of the world; that He came to save sinners. . . . [and] that He is a complete and universal Saviour.'[80] It is only through the Spirit of Truth that everything will be revealed to us: our purpose for living, our sins, and potential through restoration and cleansing. Let us also pray that the Spirit of Truth this Pentecost will purify, freshen and quicken us.

One final but vital thought for this Vigil—we must always be conscious that without the Holy Spirit there is no vitality to life in this world, and even God's actions are unrelated to us. This pulsating life of the Spirit is illustrated in this extract from an address given by the Metropolitan Ignatias of Latakia:

> Without the Holy Spirit God is far away.
>   Christ stays in the past,
>   the Gospel is simply an organization,
>   authority is a matter of propaganda,
>   the liturgy is no more than an evolution,
>   Christian loving a slave morality.
> But in the Holy Spirit
>   the cosmos is resurrected and grows
>   with the birth pangs of the Kingdom,
>   the Risen Christ is there,
>   the Gospel is the power of life,
>   the Church shows forth the life of the Trinity,
>   authority is a liberating science,
>   mission is a Pentecost,
>   the liturgy is both renewal and anticipation,
>   human action is deified.[81]

O Holy Spirit, descend upon me this Pentecost and fill me with the Spirit as You poured out upon the apostles. Just as You turned them from frightened and timid men into men of boldness and fearlessness, make me also. Let the quality of my life preach the Gospel to all. Amen.

[80] Frank, op. cit., Vol. 2, p.218.

[81] This was delivered as part of the Metropolitan Ignatias of Latakia's address to the Assembly of the World Council of Churches at Uppsala in June 1968, as printed in Ramsey, op. cit., pp.126-7.

Pentecost

The Outpouring of the Holy Spirit

The day of Pentecost had come, and they were all together in one place. Suddenly there came from the sky what sounded like a strong, driving wind, a noise which filled the whole house where they were sitting. And there appeared to them flames like tongues of fire distributed among them and coming to rest on each one. They were all filled with the Holy Spirit and began to talk in tongues.

Acts 2:1-4

Full readings: Acts 2:1-11; Psalm 104:1-2, 29-30, 34-35; 1 Corinthians 12:3-7, 12-13; St. John 20:19-23.

Nothing can contain the Spirit; it blows where it wills, and fills the whole world, renewing everything in it. Nothing is exempted from the power of His coming. How clearly we have seen this in the events in Acts. The very foundations of the prison holding Paul and Silas were shattered by an enormous earthquake while these two apostles were filled with songs of praise and thanksgiving despite their physical pain, and the gaoler and his family were baptized. Philip was directed to the Ethiopian who is resting and reading the Scriptures on his long journey home. Tabitha was raised from the dead, the slave girl was freed from the taunting evil spirits, and Paul himself was saved from certain lynching by a Jewish mob. Indeed, there is:

> no chamber so secret, but it can get into; no place so
> remote, but it can reach; none so private, but it can find;
> none so strong, but it can break through; none so deep,
> but it can fathom; none so high, but it can scale; no place
> at all, but it can come into; and none so bad, but some
> way or other it will vouchsafe to visit.[82]

The apostles as they met in prayer, which had been their custom since
Jesus departed from them ten days ago, were suddenly bombarded with
something indescribable – a mighty wind it sounded like, and in that in-
stant their lives were completely changed. Never to be the same Peter
or James or John again! They were to be the new men in Christ as He
had promised they would be when He returned to them. During these
great Fifty Days we have been reflecting on this change, and have seen
the great and wondrous works of God achieved through them. Through
them the Spirit of the Lord was filling the whole civilized world at that
time.

Pentecost means bestowing gifts. Everything we have is a gift from
the Spirit – every skill, every talent, every virtue, and every good
thought. Our understanding and wisdom, reason and knowledge, godly
fear and true godliness, counsel and spiritual strength are His gifts too.
There is nothing, but absolutely nothing that we possess that we can
claim as ours. We owe everything to His generosity of filling us each
day with so many good things. The extraordinary thing about the gifts
of the Spirit is that the more we allow them to be expressed in us, the
more gifts we shall discover we are given each day, and the more the
Lord can do through us. The riches of the Spirit's giving is un-
fathomable; they pass all human understanding. If we but realize that
we owe everything to Him, our lives would flow with gratitude, joy and
above all humility. It would also take away any feeling of inadequacies
or being nervous and tense about doing 'my best', because we know
that 'my best' is what the Holy Spirit is doing through me. We are His
instrument; it is He who is actually the artist! That is why one of the
saddest things in life is to see how many, many souls inhibit the gifts of
the Spirit. When we say that 'this person has so much potential, if
only!', what we are really saying is something like this, 'if only the Spirit
with His manifold gifts could be manifested in that person's life.'

As wonderful as all these gifts are, there is one yet more glorious
than all of these together. That gift is to be able to believe in the Lord

Jesus Christ, so that we can indeed receive grace. 'No one can say "Jesus is Lord!" except under the influence of the Holy Spirit.' (1 Cor. 12:3). Thus it is the Spirit within us which draws us from darkness into His most marvellous light. In this light we are given the perception to see ourselves as tarnished with so much dross, and the propensity to have our tarnished image cleaned. In other words, we are given grace to acknowledge our need for a Saviour. This is what prompted the gaoler to ask Paul 'What must I do to be saved?' (Acts 16:30). Once we are able to accept in our hearts that Christ is the Lord of our lives, then we welcome Love simultaneously. Possessing Christ, through the gift of the Spirit, brings also Love, Truth, Light and Life. In possessing these, there is absolutely nothing else we need. Little wonder then this is the greatest gift we can be given, to believe in Christ and His teachings. And it is no marvel that St. Paul in his writings uses the phrase 'in Christ', over and over again. Next time you are reading his letters, keep this thought in mind.

Lancelot Andrewes described Pentecost as being 'the feast of love', the *festum charitatis*, the day on which He bestows some gifts upon His people. The Spirit is 'sent to be the union, love and love- knot of the natures united in Christ; even of God with man.'[83] On this feast of Love, Andrewes equated the giving of love with the work of love as expressed in the Eucharist, 'the feast of Love, upon the feast day of Love'.

> And of His fruits the very first is love.... Now to work love, the undoubted both sign and means of His dwelling, what better way, or how sooner wrought, than by the sacrament of love; as the feast of love, upon the feast day of love; when love descended with both His hands full of gifts, for very love to take up His dwelling within us....
> He left us the gifts of His Body and Blood. His Body broken, and full of the characters of love all over. His Blood shed, every drop whereof is a great drop of love.... His Body the Spirit of strength, His Blood the Spirit of comfort; both the Spirit of love.[84]

One last thought for our reflection upon this day of gifts: Pentecost we have always associated with the liturgical colour of red as symbolizing the burning flames of fire which descended upon the gathered assembly. However, in the Orthodox Churches the liturgical colour for this feast is green, the colour of creation. By Pentecost the countryside is indeed exploding in all its greenness, every kind of tree is now mantled in its fresh green dress. Thus we are reminded that it is not only we human beings who are charged through the indwelling of the Spirit, but indeed all of God's creation. It is the living Spirit who from the beginning has filled everything with His goodness and beauty. As Hopkins so rightly says:

> The whole world is charged with the grandeur of God.
> It will flame out, like shining from shook foil;
> It gathers to a greatness, like the ooze of oil
> Crushed.[85]

The other Christian tradition which has always identified closely with God ever present in His creation is the Celtic. Indeed, the Spirit within mankind and the natural world fuses. We are becoming more and more aware of this as more early and medieval Celtic poetry is being translated from its original tongue. In this early Celtic poem, appropriately called *Benediction*, this is clearly illustrated.

> Glorious Lord, I give You greeting!
> Let the church and the chapel praise You,
> Let the chapel and the church praise You.
> Let the plain and the hillside praise You,
> Let the world's three well-springs praise You,
> Two above wind and one above land,
> Let the dark and the daylight praise You.
> Abraham, founder of faith, praised You;
> Let the life everlasting praise You,
> Let the birds and honeybees praise You,
> Let the shorn stems and the shoots praise You,
> Both Aaron and Moses praised You:
> Let the male and female praise You,
> Let the seven days and the stars praise You,
> Let the air and the ether praise You,
> Let the books and the letters praise You,
> Let the fish in the swift streams praise You,
> Let the thought and the action praise You,

Let the sand-grains and earth-clods praise You,
Let all the good that's performed praise You,
And I shall praise You, Lord of Glory:
Glorious Lord, I give You greeting![86]

As Celtic poetry is full of the spontaneity of life, given by the Spirit, I would also like to share with you a verse from another poem, *The Skylark*; this one comes from the medieval period.

Let each good creature praise his
Creator, pure radiant Lord.
Praising God as He bade you,
Thousands listen, do not cease.
Lyrist of love, where are you?
Lucid voice in garb of grey.
Your song is sweet and merry,
Melodious russet muse.
Chanter of heaven's chapel,
Fair is faith, great is Your skill.
All honour, harmonious song,
Broad is your cap, brown-tufted.[87]

So it is the Spirit which renews, replenishes, revitalizes every part of creation, what we call the natural world and us human beings. Both are intrinsically linked through the living Spirit. That is why Christians must always take an active role of caring for nature, and seek others to do likewise. Just as our own bodies are the temple for the Spirit so every branch, every flower, every bird, every mountain and every lake are also.

As we unite ourselves to Love today at the altar rail, let us pray fervently that the Spirit of the living God may fall afresh on us. On this day of gifts, let us also bring a gift to Him–ourselves–but let that gift of ourselves be emptied of self, in order to be filled with the Spirit.

On this day of gifts, fill me, O Blessed Spirit, with those gifts You know I need to be Yours in this world. Help me to grow in the fruits of the Spirit: humility, patience, long-suffering and love. I pray that I may simply be a vessel for you to replenish over and over again with Your gifts in order to proclaim Christ as Lord of the universe. Amen.

[82] Ramsey, op. cit., p.190.

[83] Andrewes, op. cit., Vol. 3, p.113.

[84] Ibid., pp.238-9.

[85] G.M. Hopkins, *The Poetical Works of Gerard Manley Hopkins*, ed. Robert Bridges (London, 1918), p.26.

[86] J.P. Clancy, *The Earliest Welsh Poetry* (London, 1970), p.113.

[87] J.P. Clancy, *Medieval Lyrics*, p.87.

Trinity Sunday

The Blessed and Undivided Trinity

The grace of the Lord Jesus Christ,
and the love of God, and the
fellowship of the Holy Spirit,
be with you all.

2 Corinthians 13:14

Full readings: Exodus 34:4-6, 8-9; Daniel 3:52-6 (as responsorial psalm); 2 Corinthians 13:11-14; St. John 3:16-18.

We worship as Christians a God who is Three in One, and One in Three, what we call the Trinity. In a sense on Trinity Sunday we celebrate the fulfilling of the functions of the Three Persons within the Godhead: Father as Creator, Son as Redeemer and the Holy Spirit as Sanctifier. Yet, each never functions alone; each Person shares in creation, redemption and sanctification.

When we become Christians we are baptized in the name of the Blessed Trinity. Furthermore, we know that the main tenet of the Christian Faith as expressed in the Creed of St. Athanasius is to 'worship one God in Trinity, and the Trinity in Unity'. This Three in One and One in Three sometimes poses problems for us, but then it is meant to because it is one of the great mysteries of our faith, and we are not meant to be able to understand everything. If we did we would then be as God, and that is not why we were created. The Orthodox hymn to the Trinity unfolds this mystery in the context of our worshipping God.

157

Let us sing praises to the Trinity,
glorifying the eternal Father,
the Son and the Spirit of righteousness,
one single Essence that we magnify in threefold song:
Holy, Holy, Holy are You, O Trinity.

I sing the praises of the three Persons in one Godhead;
I proclaim one simple Nature undivided:
Father eternal, Son and Holy Spirit,
one in throne and lordship, one single Kingdom,
one everlasting Power.

O simple and undivided Trinity, one consubstantial na-
ture:
You are praised as light and lights, one holy and three
holies.
Sing, O my soul, and glorify
Life and lives, the God of all.[88]

Yet we do have insight into this great mystery through not only the
set readings for Trinity but in that wonderful mystical Gospel of St.
John. We have been touching on it in our readings recently, where Our
Lord in His long discourse stated clearly the relationship within the
Godhead. He promises that the Spirit of Truth will reveal everything to
those who believe. 'I am in the Father and the Father in me'; 'I am not
myself the source of the words I speak to you: it is the Father who
dwells in me doing His own work'; 'when the advocate has come, whom
I shall send you from the Father–the Spirit of truth that issues from the
Father–He will bear witness to me.' (Jn. 14:10-11, 15:26).

On this Trinity Sunday, like Julian of Norwich, let the Trinity fill 'me
full of heartfelt joy', and like her be assured 'that all eternity was like this
for those who attain heaven.' According to her vision, Julian continued:

For the Trinity is God; the Trinity is our maker; the
Trinity is our keeper; the Trinity is our everlasting lover;
the Trinity is our endless joy and our bliss, by our Lord
Jesus Christ, and in our Lord Jesus Christ. . . . For when
Jesus appears, the blessed Trinity is understood as unto my
sight.[89]

This Trinity is the subject of our continual praise and thanksgiving, not of our trying to fathom its mystery. When we think on the Trinity, all of Its wonderful gifts simply overwhelm us; the sheer grandeur of it is too much for the human mind to comprehend as through the Trinity every conceivable gift and blessing has been bestowed on us. We are indeed 'lost in wonder, love and praise', conveyed in this seventeenth century poem *Trinity Sunday*, written in the style of George Herbert:

> Grace, Wit and Art, assist me; for I see
> The subjects of this day's solemnity
> So far excels in worth,
> That sooner may
> I drain the sea,
> Or drive the day
> With light away,
> Than fully set it forth,
> Except join all three to take my part,
> And chiefly Grace fill both my head and heart.
>
> Stay, busy soul, presume not to enquire
> Too much of what Angels can but admire,
> And never comprehend:
> The Trinity
> In Unity
> And Unity,
> In Trinity,
> All reason doth transcend.
> God the Father, Son God, and God Holy Ghost,
> Who most admireth, magnifieth most.
>
> And who most magnifies best understands,
> And best expresses what the heads, and hands,
> And hearts, of all men living,
> When most they try
> To glorify,
> And raise on high,
> Fall short, and lie,
> Grovelling below: Man's giving
> Is but restoring by retail, with loss,
> What from His God he first received in gross.

Faith must perform the office of invention,
And Elocution, struck with apprehension
   Of wonder silence keep.
     Not tongues, but eyes
     Lift to the skies

     Best solemnize
   This day: whereof the deep
Mysterious subject lies out of the reach
Of wit to learn, much more of Art to teach.

Then write non Ultra; *Look not for leave*
To speak of what thou never canst conceive
   Worthily, as thou shouldest:
     And it shall be
     Enough for thee,
     If none but he
     Himself doth see,
   Though thou canst not, thou wouldst
Make his praise glorious, who is alone
Thrice blessed one in three,·and three in one.[90]

We have so much for which to be eternally grateful to the blessed and undivided Trinity. Let us see the whole world in which we live and of which we are part as witnessing for the Three in One and the One in Three. The glorious Godhead does indeed shine forth from His world.

O Blessed and Holy Trinity, I praise You for You are everpresent in Your world, and I especially praise You for my creation, redemption and sanctification. May I always glorify You, Father Son and Holy Spirit, One God for ever and ever. Amen.

[88] The Lenten Triodion, trans. by Mother Mary and Archimandrite Ware (London, 1978), pp.340, 405, 473.
[89] Mother Julian of Norwich, op. cit., p.13.
[90] Herbert, op. cit., Vol. 2, pp.351-2.

Corpus et Sanguis Christi

The Blessed Sacrament

'I am the living bread that has come down from heaven;
if anyone eats this bread he will live for ever. The bread
which I shall give is my own flesh, given for the life of the
world.'

St. John 6:51

Full readings: Deuteronomy 8:2-3, 14-16; Psalm 147:12- 20; 1 Corinthians 10:16-17; St. John 6:51-8.

Now that we have finished our celebrations for the last fifty days in
honour of the Resurrection, Ascension and the coming of the Spirit at
Pentecost, we can now give due celebration for the institution of the
Blessed Sacrament, and give It the honour It so richly deserves. Our
dear Lord returned to His Father on Ascension Day, but before
returning He gave us the most wonderful gift that we can receive
daily–Himself, the Body and Blood under the guise of bread and wine.
He truly has not left us comfortless, but has blessed us with the most
precious jewel in all the world. That moment when we kneel and
receive Our Lord each day is the most wonderful of the entire day. It is
a tiny foretaste of heaven when we shall be with Our Blessed Saviour
for ever. There at the altar rail we receive the Living Christ whose Life
penetrates every inch of our being, and as it does giving us Strength,
Vitality and Love to drive out all that is not pure and lovely and whole.
It is only in the Living Christ that we can be His instruments in
this world to overcome hatred with love, jealousy with self-sacrifice,

violence with gentleness, arrogance with humility, bitterness with generosity, and disease with healing. It is, as St. Augustine put it quite crudely, 'by eating the Body of Christ, we can be the body of Christ.'

Our Lord promised that 'He who eats my bread will never hunger'. If only Christians believed this then they would come and receive His gift more often, they would run to it! Just as no other name but the name of Jesus will save us, so no other food will strengthen us, to be fit members of His kingdom and to enable us to live with Christ for ever. What more do we need? What more assurance do we want, than that from Our Lord Himself? 'As the living Father sent me, and I live because of the Father, so whoever eats me will live because of me.' (Jn. 6:57).

Yet in the receiving of this Sacrament. St. Paul gives us sober warning. We must never come to receive the Bread of Heaven without due preparation. Although we are never worthy sufficiently to receive Our Blessed Lord, nevertheless there is a big difference between acknowledging this unworthiness and preparing ourselves to be as receptive as we can, and a careless and casual approach with no real thought as to whom we are receiving and little reverence for Him. So St. Paul warns those with the latter approach that if we receive the Bread of Heaven and the Cup of Salvation unworthily then we are 'guilty of offending against the body and blood of the Lord' (1 Cor. 11:27, 29). Indeed, we do this to the damnation of our own souls. He insists that we examine ourselves if we want to escape this kind of judgment.

Just as we want to come in as worthily fashion as possible, so we want to leave by giving our heartfelt thanks for having received so freely the most wonderful gift possible. This prayer of thanksgiving from the Gallican tradition, expresses this so aptly.

> Lord Jesus, I give You thanks,
> not only with the lips and heart,
> which often comes to little, but with the spirit,
> with which I speak to You, question You,
> love You, and recognise You.
> You are my all, and everything is in You.
> In You we live, and move, and have our being.[91]

The Epistle for Corpus Christi points us to Christ in the Sacrament of the altar as the point of unity for all who receive Him. 'It is the one loaf of which we all partake.' (1 Cor. 10:17). Christ is the Head of the

Church, the Christian community, of which we are all members by virtue of our baptism. That means we are all united and bonded through Christ and in Christ. That pious prelate of the Elizabethan and Jacobean Churches, Lancelot Andrewes, described the Eucharist as the *locus* of unity, or 'the Sacrament of *accord*', manifested first by the apostles as they broke bread with one accord. 'This Sacrament of *breaking of bread* is the Sacrament of *accord*, as that which represents unto us perfect unity in the many grains kneaded into *one loaf*, and the many grapes pressed into one cup.'[92] We too have to learn to be like the apostles and break bread with one accord, and let the Fraction absorb all our disharmonies and divisions because we are indeed meant to share 'the cup of blessing' (1 Cor. 10:16). I am convinced if we loved Our Lord in His Sacrament then we would do far more about sharing this Sacrament at the same altar by all Christians.

For me one of the loveliest ways to be near Our Lord, and simply to absorb His presence and His love, is to love Him dearly in the Sacrament of the altar. Indeed, as I conclude this meditation I have just returned from Benediction. For me this is one of the most wonderful ways we can enter into the mystery and loveliness of Jesus giving Himself under the veil of Bread and Wine. 'O taste and see how gracious the Lord is' is so true when one kneels there in absorbed adoration and awe before one's Lord! I always find I don't want to leave and go out to the reality of the kind of world in which we live, but simply to linger and, like Mary, be content to sit at His feet silently but assuredly. 'Let us for ever adore the most Holy Sacrament.' If you have never tasted the delight of Heaven here upon earth, it is always there in the presence of Jesus upon the altar. To help you to be transported heavenward here is part of that beautiful Corpus Christi sequence which is sung upon this most glorious feast.

> Sing today, the mystery showing
> Of the living, life bestowing
> Bread from heaven before you set;
>
> . . .
>
> Full and clear ring out your chanting,
> Joy nor sweetest grace be wanting
> To your heart and soul today;
> When we gather up the measure

Of that Supper and its treasure,
Keeping feast in glad array.

Lo the new King's Table gracing,
This new Passover of blessing
Has fulfilled the elder rite:
Now the new, the old effaces,
Truth revealed the shadows chases,
Day is breaking on the night.

. . .

This the truth to Christians given
Bread becomes His flesh from heaven,
Wine becomes His holy blood.
Does it pass your comprehending?
Yet by Faith, your sight transcending,
Wondrous things are understood.

. . .

Whoso of this Food partakes,
Christ divides not nor breaks
He is whole to all who taste.

. . .

O true Bread, good Shepherd tend us,
Jesu, of Your love befriend us,
You refresh us, You defend us,
Your eternal goodness send us
In the land of life to see.[93]

Yet our feet must come back to earth; we must go out into the world.
That is the essential purpose for receiving God's gift of Himself. 'Send
us out into the world to live and work to Your glory' is what we are
instructed to do by the celebrant at each Mass. One of the best features
of the modern Liturgy is that the dismissal follows immediately after the
Communion. We are fed in order to be sent. We must be the Body of
Christ in this world: loving, healing, forgiving, reconciling and em-
pathizing with all.

O Jesus, in this most wonderful Sacrament of the altar, may I always love and reverence You in this special way You give Yourself to us. Help me to be truly thankful for the gift of Your Life each day, and may that Life within draw others to know and love You, as I serve You in this world. Amen.

[91] Berselli, op. cit., p.128.

[92] Andrewes, op. cit., Vol. 3, p.128.

[93] St. Thomas Aquinas in *The New English Hymnal*, op. cit., pp.783-9.

An Easter Litany

Christ is Risen. Alleluia! Alleluia! Alleluia!
He is risen indeed. Alleluia! Alleluia! Alleluia!

Spring bursts today
For Christ is risen and all the earth's at play.

Flash, forth, thou Sun,
The rain is over and gone, its work is done.

Winter is past,
Sweet Spring is come at last, is come at last.

Bud, Fig and Vine
Bud, Olive, fat with fruit and oil and wine.

Break forth this morn
In roses, thou but yesterday a thorn.

Uplift thy head,
O pure white Lily through the Winter dead.

Beside your dams
Leap and rejoice, you merry-making Lambs.

All Herds and Flocks
Rejoice, all Beasts of thickets and of rocks.

Sing creatures, sing
Angels and Men and Birds and everything.

All notes of Doves
Fill all our world: this is the time of love.[94]

On this most triumphant day we praise and thank You for Your victory over death and assuring us of life beyond the grave.

On this most triumphant day we praise and thank You for Your victory over sin and releasing us from the sin of the first Adam.

On this most triumphant day we praise and thank You for Your victory over the servitude we inherit from sin and giving us a new life in the second Adam.

On this most triumphant day we praise and thank You for Your victory over all darkness and illuminating us with your Light.

On this most triumphant day we praise and thank You for Your victory over all evil and filling us with the Spirit of truth.

On this most triumphant day we praise and thank You for Your victory over our corruptions and restoring us to our potential.

On this most triumphant day we praise and thank You for Your victory over all sham and opening to us the joy and delights of Your kingdom.

Christ has risen from the grave. Alleluia! Alleluia! Alleluia!

And has become the first fruits of all those who have died. Alleluia! Alleluia! Alleluia!

For since it was a man who brought death into the world, a man also brought resurrection of the dead. As in Adam all die, so in Christ all will be brought to life.

(1 Cor. 15:21-2)

Let us come and meet the Risen Lord.

Mary Magdalen came with the other women to see the tomb where the Lord had been laid. The angel greeted them with the news, 'He is not here but has arisen.'

Mary Magdalen stood in the garden weeping when she is greeted with the sound of her own name, 'Mary.'

'Do not touch me,' commands Jesus, 'but go and tell my disciples I am risen and shall ascend to my Father.'

Let us come and meet the Risen Lord.

Christians, to the Paschal Victim

Offer your thankful praises.
A Lamb the sheep redeems:
Christ, who only is sinless,
Reconciles sinners to the Father.

Death and life have contended
In that combat stupendous:
The Prince of Life,
who died, reigns immortal.

Speak Mary, declaring
What you saw wayfaring:
'The Tomb of Christ, who is living,
The glory of Jesus' resurrection:
Bright angels attesting,
The shroud and napkin resting.

Yes, Christ my hope is arisen:
To Galilee He before you.'
Happy they who hear the witness
Mary's word believing
Above the tales of doubt and deceiving,

Christ indeed from death is risen.
Our new life obtaining
Have mercy, victor King, ever reigning!
Amen. Alleluia.[95]

Christ has risen from death and is alive, ever making intercessions for us in heaven. Let us join our Paschal petitions with those of our Risen Lord:

Lord, You are the light of the world. Penetrate the hearts of all those who live in darkness and make their lives a prison.

Lead all those who are the victims of other peoples' darkness — the captives and prisoners – know that Your light does in the end dispel all darkness. Be their constant companion in those hours of torture and loneliness.

Lead all those who are the victims of disease and sickness to seek enlightenment and healing from Your Risen Life.

Lord You are the Truth of the World. Teach all those who deliberately debase truth to discover the riches of being free from the tyranny of deceit.
Teach the young that in their growing up they may have a real thirst to know what is true, and the source of it.
Guide all those who teach and influence others in their professions never to pervert the Truth, but always to seek it diligently and above every other virtue.

Lord You are the Way. Guide and enrich all who have not discovered that You are the Way which leads to eternal life.
Guide all those who have fallen by the way. Restore them to the path which leads to You.
Guide all Your faithful as they follow You. Replenish them when the journey becomes wearisome and difficult and even boring.

Lord, You are Life. Give us that eternal life, so that our lives will be overbrimming with joy, cheerfulness and delight because we know that You have overcome every sting and fear in Your victory over the Cross. Amen.

  Jesus lives! thy terrors now,
   Can, O Death, no more appal us;
  Jesus lives! by this we know
   You, O grave, canst not enthral us.   Alleluia!

  Jesus lives! henceforth is death
   But the gate of life immortal;
  This shall calm our trembling breath,
   When we pass its gloomy portal.   Alleluia!

  Jesus lives! for us He died;
   Then, alone to Jesus living,
  Pure in heart may we abide,
   Glory to our Saviour giving.   Alleluia!

  Jesus lives! our hearts know well

Nought from us His love will sever;
Life, nor death, nor powers of hell
Tear us from His keeping ever.   Alleluia!

Jesus lives! to Him the throne
Over all the world is given;
May we go where He is gone,
Rest and reign with Him in heaven.   Alleluia![96]

[94] Rossetti, op. cit., p.255.
[95] The Easter Sequence in *The New English Hymnal,* op. cit., pp.778-80.
[96] Frances Cox (trans.) in *The New English Hymnal,* op. cit., pp.172-3.

Ascension Litany

God goes up with shouts of joy. Alleluia! Alleluia! Alleluia!
The Lord goes up with trumpet blast. Alleluia! Alleluia! Alleluia!

Today You are welcomed home by the Father and the angels.
Heaven rings out with their unceasing praises of welcome.

The Lord ascends up on high,
    Loud anthems round him swelling;
The Lord has triumphed gloriously,
    In power and might excelling:
Hell and the grave are captive led;
Lo, He returns, our glorious Head,
    To His eternal dwelling.

The heavens with joy receive their Lord;
    O day of exultation!
By saints, by angel-hosts adored
    For His so great salvation:
O earth, adore your glorious King,
His rising, His ascension sing
    With grateful adoration.

By saints in earth and saints in heaven,
    With songs for ever blended,
All praise to Christ our King be given,
    Who has to heaven ascended:
To Father, Son and Holy Ghost,
The God of heaven's resplendent host,
    In bright array extended.[97]

Jesus, You ascend to Your Father, and our Father, to Your God and our God.

Jesus, the King of glory, You are now seated at the right hand of Your Father.

Jesus, the Crowned Heir, You are now restored to Your rightful place in heaven.

Jesus, the High Priest, You are now forever interceding on our behalf.

Jesus, Judge and Lord of all mankind, be merciful to us on Judgment day.

Jesus, You ascend to Your Father, so that You may return to us through Your promised Spirit.

> Hail, Festival Day, blest day that is hallowed for ever;
> Day when the Lord ascends, high in the heavens to reign.
> > Alleluia! Alleluia! Alleluia!

We thank You, O King of Glory, for Your glorious Ascension.

We thank You, O King of Glory, for the hope of our own rising through Your Ascension.

We thank You, O King of Glory, for the joy of knowing You will always be with us through the Holy Spirit.

We thank You, O King of Glory, that we have You as a Mediator, between us and God the Father.

We thank You, O King of Glory, for every blessing You give us through Your Ascension.

Just as You have triumphed over all trials, O Crowned One, help us to overcome any trials and tribulations of this life.

Just as You have been victorious over sin, O Crowned One, assist us to overcome all our besetting sins.

Just as You have conquered death, O Crowned One, help us to live so that we fear the grave as little as our bed.

Just as You are now seated on Your throne, welcome us to Your home at the end of our earthly pilgrimage.

You have passed beyond our sight, but not to abandon us, but to give us hope because where You have gone we shall surely follow if we are but faithful to You. Fill us with joy and lift our hearts to You now and forever. Amen.

You are with us always, even unto the end of the world. Alleluia! Alleluia! Alleluia!

[97] A. Russell and others, in *The New English Hymnal*, op. cit., pp.203-4.

Pentecost Litany

The Spirit of the Lord fills the whole world.
Let all creation praise you. Alleluia! Alleluia! Alleluia!

O Holy Spirit, You came as a rushing, mighty wind, revitalize my whole being with that same energy.

O Holy Spirit, You came as fire, burn within me so my whole being glows with Your love.

O Holy Spirit, You came unannounced, direct me wherever You want me to go, and to do what you want.

O Holy Spirit, You came as the Comforter, support me in all my doings.

O Holy Spirit, You came as Truth, implant within me that deep desire for truth and honesty in all things.

O Holy Spirit, You came as Love, pour into my very soul that yearning to love You above everything else and my neighbour as myself.

> Holy Spirit, Lord of light,
> From the clear celestial height
>   Your pure beaming radiance give.
>
> Come, You Father of the poor,
> Come with treasures which endure
>   Come, you light of all that live!
>
> You, of all consolers best,
> You, the soul's delightful guest,
>   Do refreshing peace bestow,

You in toil are comfort sweet;
Pleasant coolness in the heat;
Solace in the midst of woe.

Light immortal, light divine,
Visit You these hearts of Yours
And our inmost being fill:

If You take Your grace away,
Nothing pure in man will stay;
All his good is turned to ill.

Heal our wounds, our strength renew;
On our dryness pour Your dew;
Wash the stains of guilt away:

Bend the stubborn heart and will;
Melt the frozen, warm the chill;
Guide the steps that go astray.

You, on us who evermore
You confess and You adore,
With Your sevenfold gifts descend:

Give us comfort when we die;
Give us life with You on high;
Give us joys that never end.

(Pentecost Sequence)

The Spirit of the Lord fills the whole world. Alleluia!
Come fill the hearts of Your people, and enkindle in them the fire of Your love.
The apostles waited and prayed for the coming of the Spirit.
Come fill the hearts of Your people, and enrich them in the knowledge of Your Word.
The apostles were transformed through the Holy Spirit. Alleluia!
Come fill the hearts of Your people, and inflame in them a missionary zeal.

You filled the early Church with strength, joy and love to serve You.
Fill the Church today with the same power, joy and love to witness for
You.

On this feast day of Love, let us pray for all those who do not know
from their own experiences what love is. And so we pray for:

* those who impoverish others through tyrannical leadership, paren-
  thood or teaching;
* those who are too frightened to show love to others;
* those who perpetuate hatred in all parts of our world;
* those who ruthlessly trample on others to get where they want in
  life;
* those who capitalize on the weaknesses of others.

Heal these people by the power of the living Christ. Amen.

A mighty wind invades the world,
So strong and free on beating wing:
It is the Spirit of the Lord
From whom all truth and freedom spring.

The Spirit is a fountain clear
For ever leaping to the sky,
Whose waters give unending life,
Whose timeless source is never dry.

The Spirit comes in tongues of flame,
With love and wisdom burning bright,
The wind, the fountain and the fire
Combine in this great feast of light.

O tranquil Spirit, bring us peace,
With God the Father and the Son.
We praise You, blessed Trinity,
Unchanging, and for ever One. Amen.[98]

The apostles were all of one accord in prayer and the breaking of Bread as they waited for Your coming. Heal the Church today of its many divisions which separate Christians from fellow Christians. Give us all a burning desire to heal Your Body, dear Lord, which we break over and over again in so many paltry ways. Just as the Spirit turns the bread and wine into Christ's Body and Blood, so transform our deadened desire for unity into a lively one. Amen.

Send forth Your power, Lord, from Your holy temple in Jerusalem, and bring to perfection Your work among us. Alleluia! Alleluia! Alleluia!

[98] From *The Divine Office, Shorter Form* (Glasgow, 1990), pp.429-30.

Trinity Litany

Glory be to the Father, and to the Son, and to the Holy Spirit; the all-ruling triune God be glory.

> I bind unto myself today
> The strong name of the Trinity,
> By invocation of the same,
> The Three in One, and One in Three.

> I bind unto myself the name,
> The strong name of the Trinity;
> By invocation of the same,
> The Three in One, and One in Three,
> Of whom all nature has creation;
> Eternal Father, Spirit, Word:
> Praise to the Lord of my salvation,
> Salvation is of Christ the Lord. Amen.[99]

O God the Father, of heaven: have mercy upon us miserable sinners.

O God the Son, redeemer of the world: have mercy upon us miserable sinners.

O God the Holy Spirit, proceeding from the Father and the Son: have mercy upon us miserable sinners.

O holy, blessed and glorious Trinity, three Persons and one God: have mercy upon us miserable sinners.

Blessed be God the Father and His only-begotten Son and the Holy Spirit: for the triune God has shown that He loves us. Alleluia!

We adore You, O blessed and undivided Trinity for the splendour of creation.

We adore You, O blessed and undivided Trinity for the continued

renewal within Your creation.
We adore You, O blessed and undivided Trinity for Your brooding over creation.

Within the blessed Trinity, there are three attributes: fatherhood, motherhood and lordship, but all in one God. You, O almighty Father, have sustained and blessed us. By Your skill and wisdom, O Second Person, we are sustained, restored and saved from our sensual nature. In You, O good Lord, the Holy Spirit, after our life and hardship is over, give us that reward which surpasses all that we can ever desire. Such is Your abounding grace and magnificent courtesy, O blessed Trinity. Amen.[100]

> Father most holy, merciful and tender;
> Jesus our Saviour, with the Father reigning;
> Spirit all kindly, Advocate, Defender,
>   Light never waning;
>
> Trinity sacred, Unity unshaken;
>   Deity perfect, giving and forgiving.
> Light of the angels, Life of the forsaken,
>   Hope all living;
>
> Maker of all things, all Your creatures praise You;
>   Lo, all things serve You through Your creation:
> Hear us, Almighty, hear us as we raise You
>   Heart's adoration.
>
> To the all-ruling triune God be glory:
>   Highest and greatest, help You our endeavour,
> We too would praise You, giving honour worthy,
>   Now and for ever. Amen.[101]

The grace of the Lord Jesus Christ, the love of God and the fellowship of the Holy Spirit be with us always. Amen. Alleluia!

---

[99] St. Patrick, *The New English Hymnal*, op. cit., pp.241-2.
[100] I have based this Prayer on the writing of Mother Julian, op. cit., pp.219-20.
[101] P. Dearmer, in *The New English Hymnal*, op. cit., p.216.

Corpus et Sanguis Christi Litany

I am the living bread which came down from heaven; whoever eats this bread will live for ever. Alleluia! Alleluia! Alleluia!

You give us bread from heaven, containing in itself all sweetness. Alleluia! Alleluia! Alleluia!

You fed Your people with the finest wheat and honey and their hunger was satisfied. Alleluia! Alleluia! Alleluia!

> O Jesus! draw me to Your beauty bright,
> O Love by You I'm rapt in ecstasy!
> O Living Love! cast me not from Your sight!
> O Love, O Love, my soul is one with You!
> > O Love, You are its Life;
> > From You it ne'er can part,
> > For You have rent my heart,
> > In such a loving strife.[102]

Soul of Christ be my sanctification.
Body of Christ be my salvation.
Blood of Christ fill all my veins.
Water of Christ's side wash out my stains.
Passion of Christ my comfort be.
O Good Jesu, listen to me.
In Your wounds I fain would hide,
Never to be parted from Your side.
Guard me should the foe assail me.
Call me when my life will fail me.

Bid me come to You above.
With Your saints to sing Your love.
For ever and ever. Amen.

Let me adore You for ever in the most holy Sacrament.

O Sacrament most holy, O Sacrament divine,
All praise and all thanksgiving
Be every moment Yours.

Let me adore You for ever in the most holy Sacrament.

Thank You, dear Lord, for giving me Your life in this wonderful
Sacrament to share with others.
Thank You, dear Lord, for giving me grace in Your Sacrament to go
out into the world to live and work for You.
Thank You, dear Lord, for feeding me with heavenly Food on my
pilgrimage to my native land.
Thank You, dear Lord, for every benefit I receive from this most
holy Sacrament. Let me never come unworthily to Your Table.

O Lord God, heavenly Father, look upon the glorious
face of Your Christ, and have mercy on me, and on all
other sinners for whom Your blessed Son our Lord
deigned to suffer death, and for whose salvation and
consolation He has chosen to remain for ever with us in
the Holy Sacrament of the Altar, and Who with You and
the Holy Spirit lives and reigns one God for ever and
ever.   Amen.[103]

The apostles were all one in the breaking of the bread.

O Sacrament of mercy!
O Sacrament of unity!
O bond of love!
He who desires life, finds here where to live,
has something to live for.
Let him draw near and believe;
let him become part of this body

and he will have life.
Let him not disdain communion with the other faithful,
not be a gangrenous member needing amputation,
not be a deformed member of which to be ashamed;
let him be complete, dignified, sound,
profoundly united with the whole body;
let him live with God, for God,
let him now work on earth
and then reign with Him in heaven.[104]

We who are many, are one body, for we all partake of the one
bread.
Let us love one another in the power of this most wonderful Sacrament.

Let us all love Our Lord in His Sacrament.
Through His life we are all brothers and sisters.

O come let us adore You, O Christ the Lord.
O come let us adore You, O Christ the Lord.
O come let us adore You, O Christ the Lord.

Alleluia! Alleluia! Alleluia! Amen.

I languish for the love of You,
For Your embraces sweet I pine;
Without Your life is death to me.
With sighs and tears this heart of mine
Craves Your return that it may be
Transformed by You, made wholly Yours.
O Love! make no delay—
O hasten unto me!
Unite me close to You,
Consume my heart away.[105]

[102] St. Francis of Assisi, op. cit., p.164.
[103] Ibid., p.167.
[104] Berselli, op. cit., p.90.
[105] St. Francis, op. cit., p.157.

Bibliography

Andrewes, L. *The Works of Lancelot Andrewes*, eds. J. Bliss and J. P. Wilson, 11 vols. (The Library of Anglo-Catholic Theology, Oxford, 1841-1854).

Arnold, D. (ed.) *Praying with The Martyrs* (London, 1991).

Bettensen, H. (ed.) *The Early Christian Fathers* (Oxford, 1990).

Bettensen, H. (ed.) *The Later Christian Fathers* (Oxford, 1989).

Berselli, C. (ed.) *To Him Be Praise*, trans. from the Italian by Sr. Mary of Jesus, O.D.C. (London, 1982).

St. Clement and St. Ignatius *The Epistles of St. Clement and St. Ignatius of Antioch* (The Works of The Fathers, London, 1946), Vol. 1.

Clancy, J. P. *Medieval Welsh Lyrics* (London, 1965).

Clancy, J. P. *The Earliest Welsh Poetry* (London, 1970).

Crashaw, R. *Crashaw's Poetical Works*, ed. I. C. Martin (Oxford, 1927).

Etchells, R. (ed.) *Praying with The English Poets* (London, 1990).

Frank, M. *Sermons Preached by Mark Frank*, 2 vols. (The Library of Anglo-Catholic Theology, Oxford, 1849).

Farindon, A. *The Sermons of Anthony Farindon*, 4 vols. (London, 1848).

Fenelon, F. *The Spiritual Letters of Archbishop Fenelon: Letters to Women*, ed. H. L. S. Lear (London, 1877).

St. Francis of Assisi. *Works of . . . St. Francis of Assisi*, trans. by a religious of that order (London, 1882).

St. Gregory Nazianzen. *The Homilies of St. Gregory Nazianzen* (Nicene and Post-Nicene Fathers of the Christian Church, Oxford, 1894), Vol. 7.

Herbert, G. *The Works of George Herbert*, 2 vols. (London, 1859).

Hildegard of Bingen. *Scivias*, trans. Mother Columba Hart and Jane Bishop (The Classics of Western Spirituality, New York, 1990).

Hilton, W. *The Scale of Perfection* (London, 1901).

Hopkins, G. M. *The Poems of Gerard Manley Hopkins*, ed. Robert Bridges (London, 1918).

Mother Julian of Norwich. *Revelations of Divine Love* (London, 1877).

Lake, A. *Sermons with Some Religious and Divine Meditations by The Right Reverend . . . Arthur Lake, Late Lord Bishop of Bath and Wells* (London, 1629).

Merton, T. *The Power and Meaning of Love* (London, 1976).

Newman, J. H. *Parochial and Plain Sermons*, 8 vols. (London, 1868).

St. Polycarp. *The Epistles and Martyrdom of St. Polycarp* (The Works of The Fathers, London, 1948), Vol. 6.

Ramsey, M. *Holy Spirit* (London, 1977).

Rolle, R. *Selected Works of Richard Rolle*, ed. G. C. Heseltine (London, 1930).

Rossetti, C. *The Poetical Works of Christina Georgina Rossetti, with Memoir and Notes by W. M. Rossetti* (London, 1904).

Runcie, R. and Hume, B. *Prayers For Peace* (London, 1987).

Spenser, E. *Poetical Works of Edmund Spenser* (Oxford, 1912).

Taylor, J. *The Whole Works of the Rt. Rev'd. Jeremy Taylor*, ed. C. P. Eden, 10 vols. (London, 1844-1853).

Tutu, D. *Hope and Suffering* (London, 1984).

Williams, R. D. *The Truce of God* (London, 1983).

Hymnals and Service Books:

The New English Hymnal, Melody Edition (Norwich, 1988).

The Lenten Triodion (London, 1978).

The Divine Office (The Shorter Form, Glasgow, 1990).